FILM ANIMATION TECHNIQUES

A Beginner's Guide and Handbook

D1709730

FILM ANIMATION TECHNIQUES

A Beginner's Guide and Handbook

Lafe Locke

BETTERWAY BOOKS
CINCINNATI, OHIO

Film Animation Techniques: A Beginner's Guide and Handbook. Copyright
© 1992 by Lafe Locke. Printed and bound in the United States of America.
All rights reserved. No part of this book may be reproduced in any form or
by any electronic or mechanical means including information storage and
retrieval systems without permission in writing from the publisher, except
by a reviewer, who may quote brief passages in a review. Published by Betterway Books, an imprint of F&W Publications, Inc., 1507 Dana Avenue,
Cincinnati, Ohio 45207. 1-800-289-0963. This book was originally published
as *Techniques for Film Animation* (J. Weston Walch, Publisher, 1985). This
edition has been revised and updated.

97 96 95 94 93   5 4 3 2

Library of Congress Cataloging in Publication Data

Locke, Lafe
    Film animation techniques : a beginner's guide and handbook / Lafe
Locke.
    p. cm.
    Includes bibliographical references and index.
    ISBN 1-55870-236-9 (pbk)
    1. Animation (Cinematography) I. Title
TR897.5.L63 1992
778.5'347 — dc20   91-43783
                                                            CIP

Cover design by Lafe Locke

Illustrations by Lafe Locke

Prepress services by Studio 500 Associates

QUANTITY DISCOUNTS AVAILABLE

This and other Betterway Books are available at a discount when purchased
in bulk. Schools, organizations, corporations and others interested in purchasing bulk quantities of this book should contact the SPECIAL SALES
DEPARTMENT of F&W Publications at 1-800-289-0963 (8 A.M.-5 P.M.
Eastern Time) or write to this department at 1507 Dana Avenue, Cincinnati, OH 45207.

CONTENTS

INTRODUCTION

Stop! Before you start reading this book, watch a bit of basic animation.

Hold this book firmly in your left hand at about the middle of the spine. Grasp the right edge, with your thumb on top. Now riffle the pages from front to back and watch the right margins. Go ahead, we'll wait.

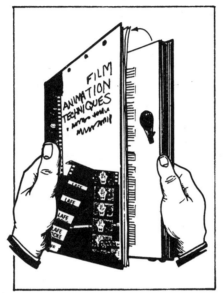

Fig. 1 *Hold the book like this and riffle the pages.*

Did you see the balloon go up?

You were witnessing an example of one of the earliest forms of animation developed for entertainment — the simple *flip book*. We'll talk about flip books and several other forms of animation in this manual. They all have one thing in common. Each is made up of a series of unmoving (still) photographs or drawings. By looking at the pictures one after another in rapid succession, you get the impression that they are "animated"; that is, that they are moving pictures. You don't actually see them move; you just think you do. As a matter of fact, your mind's eye doesn't have

time to perceive each still picture as a separate unit. Instead, it registers a series of overlapping impressions; thus, an animated ball bounces, a girl waves, an elephant flies, and, as in the margins of this book, the little balloon goes up.

It is this now-you-see-it, now-you-don't phenomenon that makes film animation so fascinating — and so useful. Because it tricks you as does a sleight-of-hand artist, animation can do the "impossible" things that live-action motion pictures can't do. That's why, whether you're aware of it or not, you see one or more forms of animation just about every time you see a television commercial. The top unscrews itself from a steak sauce bottle. Two laundry product containers merge into one. A cartoon lion talks to real kids at the breakfast table. And product names fly on and off the screen, expand, contract, and do flip-flops.

Wouldn't you like to do things like that yourself? We don't mean expand, contract, and do flip-flops. We mean wouldn't you like to make animated films of cartoons, objects, and words so that *they* will do visual acrobatics?

Read and follow the directions in this book and you can.

The animation you see on your television and at the movie theater is produced by skilled animators, using highly sophisticated techniques and equipment. But that shouldn't stop you from finding fun and purpose in animation. There are ways to make animated films that are relatively easy for beginners. (You can even get by without using a camera.)

This book is devoted to showing you how to use those easy animation methods, the ones that require a minimum of equipment and very little expense. If an animation technique calls for complicated or costly equipment, you won't find it outlined in this book. After you've mastered the fundamentals that you learn here, you can step up to more advanced animation techniques.

So, get moving! On film!

1

WHAT MAKES MICKEY MOUSE MOVE?

If you have ever examined a strip of animation film, or a regular motion picture film for that matter, you know that it is made up of a series of stationary (still) pictures. Each picture is in its own *frame*; and, if the people or objects in the filmed sequence are supposed to be moving, their positions are slightly different in each subsequent frame on the strip of film. Only when the film is projected and you see the individual pictures in rapid succession do you get the illusion of motion.

In fact, the projector in which the film is shown is designed to ensure that you'll see only one picture at a time (Figure 2). It allows a certain number of the framed pictures to pass each second in front of an opening called a *film-gate*. The frames don't move smoothly through the projector, however. Instead, they are jerked forward one at a time, and each frame stops in front of the film-gate. The *gate* opens, allowing the frame to be projected onto the viewing screen, then shuts again for a tiny instant until the next frame is jerked in front of it.

Thus, when you watch a movie screen showing, for example, a Mickey Mouse cartoon, you are actually seeing a sequence of static pictures alternating with a blacked-out screen. Because all this happens so fast (18 times per second for silent films and 24 times per second for films with sound tracks), you are not aware of the blank periods on the screen any more than you are aware of your vision being blacked out every time you blink your eyes.

How, then, do you see Mickey Mouse jump and run? How do you get the illusion of motion when you actually are seeing a series of stationary pictures?

PERSISTENCE OF VISION

The answer to that question also explains why you don't see the blacked-out portions of the film. It is called *persistence of vision*. This is a remarkable ability of the human eye to keep an image in view for a split second after the image has been removed from sight. Thus, the still pictures you see on the screen are overlapping in your consciousness. Image blends into image, and you get the optical illusion of movement from pictures that really aren't moving at all. Without persistence of vision, you would simply see hundreds or thousands of quickly projected still pictures — a pretty jerky experience, indeed.

ANALYZING MOVEMENTS

A practical approach to understanding animation is to analyze some simple *action*. By noting and isolating the different positions of a moving object, you can more easily see how the film animator puts them back together again in a sequence of pictures that comes alive on the screen.

You have one example before you at this very instant, with one frame of the animation already isolated for you. It is the little balloon in the margin of this page. Note that an identical balloon is positioned in the margin of the next right-hand page, another is even higher on the page after that, and so on. When the pages are riffled, the series of stationary pictures looks like one balloon going up. That's your persistence of vision at work. We will go into this type of flip book animation in more detail in Chapter 4.

Another aid to understanding motion is to examine *stroboscopic* photographs (Figure 3). Perhaps your library has in its art or photography sections one or more books that show examples of *strobe* photos of running athletes, ballet dancers, trotting horses, falling cats (they always land on their feet), and so on. These overlapping photographs show, in effect,

Fig. 2 In animation, as in regular motion pictures, you see only one still picture at a time.

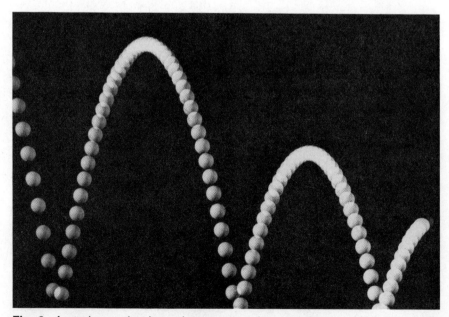

Fig. 3 A stroboscopic photo demonstrates how persistence of vision makes animated images overlap in your mind's eye.

what happens in your mind's eye when you watch an animated film. Your persistence of vision merges one image with the next.

Incidentally, it's a good idea to have a book of stroboscopic photos available for reference. Later on, when you are actually making animated films, the pictures can serve as excellent guides for planning sequences of action.

AN EXERCISE IN MOTION

It is time to start getting some of your own work into the act. By making a cutout paper puppet and manipulating its moving parts, you can create your own application of animated movement. The puppet will be your model for making static drawings of the several stages in a single motion. Later on, when you have progressed to actual filming, you may wish to use the puppet itself in a film.

Draw your own puppet, using any type of person or animal that strikes your fancy. This will put you one

Fig. 4

HINGES CAN BE MADE OF WIRE. BEND PRONGS FLAT AFTER INSERTING THROUGH HOLES.

ASSEMBLE WITH STATIONERY HINGES

Fig. 5 How the cutout jogger parts are assembled.

Fig. 6 *Chart the jogger's movements and you get what looks like a stroboscopic photo.*

step ahead when you start to make cutout figures for animation (Chapter 10). Be sure to keep your drawing simple, remembering that parts of it will have to be moved. A few added lines of detail can give "character" to your puppet, but this is not necessary at this time.

We'll use a "jogger" (Figure 4) to serve as a guide in making a puppet. Here's how to go about it:

1. Draw your puppet about 7 inches (18cm) tall on a piece of paper. Since parts of it will change position (at knees, elbows, shoulders, etc.), indicate clearly where the separate moving parts will have to be overlapped for joining. (See dotted lines on Figure 4.) This jogger has only seven parts, because movement at the elbows and neck has been eliminated to simplify the puppet.

2. Trace the individual parts onto stiff paper or cardboard. A two-ply or three-ply white Bristol board, available at art supply stores, is ideal for this.

3. Cut out all the pieces. Punch holes at the joints and assemble your puppet with paper fasteners (Figure 5). Be sure the parts will move easily.

4. Place your puppet flat on a large sheet of white paper and trace around it, using a sharp pointed pencil, pen, or felt marker. Then move the puppet slightly up, down, or to either side according to the direction in which you want it to move. Change the position of the arms and legs appropriate to the action, and trace around the entire puppet again. Move the puppet slightly to a new position, adjusting the arms and legs again, and make another outline. Continue in this manner until you have a succession of overlapping drawings (Figure 6) similar to a stroboscopic photo.

Correctly done, your composite drawing is now actually a "blueprint" of a simple sequence of movements by your puppet. Each separate outline could now be copied on a separate sheet to be used as a frame in a very simplified animated film.

A SLIDE DEMONSTRATION

For a further demonstration of how a series of static pictures can be made

to give the illusion of movement, try transferring the puppet sequence you have just drawn to 35mm slides for use in a tray or carousel projector.

An economical way to do this, and fun in the bargain, is to draw the individual outlines of the puppet directly on small pieces of tracing paper or clear *acetate* (plastic sheeting), available at art supply stores. Use pen and ink or a fine-point felt-tipped marker labeled "permanent."

Each drawing should be no larger than 1 1/4" x 3/4" (32 x 20 mm). Allow enough margin around each drawing for framing. Mount these in standard 2" x 2" (35mm) cardboard slide frames, available at camera shops. Number your slides in the correct sequence and put them into the projector tray.

A more impressive way to obtain the slides is to trace the puppet figures you did for the previous exercise in making cutouts. Trace each figure on a separate sheet of paper, filling in the details of the jogger if you wish. Then photograph the drawings for slides.

Once you have your slides made, show them in a projector with the ability to make rapid slide changes. This will project them fast enough to provide a semblance of the desired illusion of motion that animation is all about. You can add to the length of your slide show by simply repeating the sequence of drawings on additional slides. However, the purpose of this exercise is not to produce finished or lengthy animation but to acquaint you with its most fundamental elements.

But look what you've done! You have already progressed from merely observing to drawing on paper and projecting what you drew. Now, let's move on to even more animated discussions.

2

HOW FILM ANIMATION DEVELOPED

What does an ancient Greek soldier spinning his shield in the light of a campfire have in common with Daffy Duck? They both illustrate one of man's age-old ambitions. As long as human beings have had pictures, they have desired to make the pictures move.

It might even be said that pictures were devised in an effort to show how things move. Back when Neanderthal artists were scratching drawings on cave walls, there were attempts to show the action of the hunt. Wall paintings 30,000 years old, discovered in Spain and France, depict consecutive and sometimes overlapping drawings of animals. Extra legs, superimposed one on the other, show the different leg positions of the animals' running action.

This storytelling by sequential images has been a method of human communication in all of recorded history. Orientals have had shadow puppet shows for many centuries. We can still see stories in bas-relief on Greek temples, Egyptian funereal paintings, medieval stained glass, and, of course, the Sunday comics.

It isn't known just when some prehistoric Walt Disney got the idea of getting the illusion of motion by moving the pictures themselves. But it is known that ancient Greek and Roman soldiers had learned how to entertain their companions by turning their round shields into animation

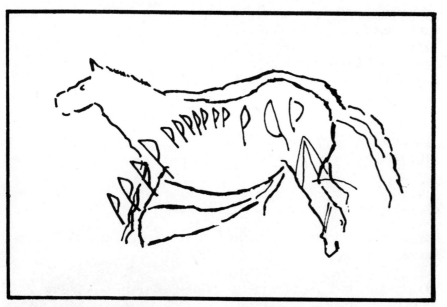

Fig. 7 *This horse, running to escape a boomerang-like weapon, was painted on a cave wall at Les Trois Frères, France, sometime before 10,000 B.C. The prehistoric "animator" used duplicate images to show motion.*

Fig. 8 *A typical magic lantern like this one thrilled early fairgoers with projected images.*

devices. They painted silhouette figures in various positions around a shield's margin, then spun the shield like a wheel while their audience stared at a fixed point. This same principle was used centuries later in devices that created a sensation in public and home entertainment.

EARLY ATTEMPTS AT ANIMATION

But alas, nobody gave animated pictures much serious thought until early

Fig. 9 *A Thaumatrope, one of the first attempts at animating drawings, was easier to make than to spell.*

in the seventeenth century. Then, in 1640, Althanasius Kircher, a Jesuit, invented a "magic lantern" capable of projecting drawings, greatly enlarged, upon a wall. It was very near in concept to our modern slide projectors. Fra Kircher and a fellow monk, Gaspar Schott, developed a crude "filmstrip," a straight strip of pictures that could be moved through the magic lantern to tell a story. Schott later modified this design, putting the individual drawings around the perimeter of a revolving disc. As the Greek and Roman soldiers did, remember?

A century later, Schott's idea impressed a Dutch scientist, Pieter Van Musschenbroek. In 1736 he established what turned out to be a working model for modern animation films by creating and projecting a series of drawings of a revolving windmill. Each drawing showed the windmill vanes in a different position so that, when the pictures were projected in rapid succession, the vanes appeared to be turning.

Meanwhile, wandering showmen were common sights at fairs and markets as they traveled from town to town presenting magic lantern shows. Their spectacles were extremely crude by today's standards. But, considering the fact that their audiences had never so much as imagined that a larger-than-life picture could be projected on a wall — or a bedsheet — the magic lantern shows were nothing less than super-extravaganzas in their day.

One man, at least, observed them with the eye of a scientist. He was Peter Mark Roget, a Londoner of Swiss birth whom we know because of the thesaurus he compiled. In 1825 Roget published a treatise titled, "Persistence of Vision with Regard to Moving Objects." It explained the scientific principle underlying the popular and growing entertainment fad.

Roget's study encouraged others to get into the act and directly influenced some of the ensuing developments. But already the phenomenon of "moving" pictures was taking an interesting side road. Inspired by the magic lantern shows at fairs and other public gatherings, the search had moved to the development of individual viewing devices and other "optical toys" for home entertainment.

THE THAUMATROPE

An early invention of this type was the *Thaumatrope*, perhaps the simplest of the lot, invented in the 1820s by an English doctor, John Paris. Despite its imposing name, the Thaumatrope was nothing more than a small disc with an image drawn on one side and another image on the opposite side. Two short threads were attached to the sides of the disc (Figure 9) so that it could be spun by blowing on the disc or twirling the threads between the fingers. Thanks to persistence of vision, the two images appeared to combine. Example: A monkey is on one side and an empty cage on the other. When the disc spins, the monkey appears to be in the cage. Though extremely elemental, this little device was a significant step in the development of motion pictures.

A person directly influenced by Roget's explanation of persistence of vision was a Belgian artist-scientist, Joseph Plateau. He developed an optical gadget called the *Phenakistoscope* (Figure 10). Because of a "shutter" principle it employed, this machine is said to be the great-grandaddy of the modern motion picture projector.

Plateau mounted sixteen pictures around the rim of a spinning disc. (Those Greek and Roman shields keep popping up, don't they?) The viewer looked through an opening that restricted the view to one picture at a time, but produced the illusion of action. You can easily make your own version of the Phenakistoscope, using a single disc with slotted openings around the rim, plus a mirror.

Talk about popularity! Plateau's gadget and other variations took off like Hula Hoops and computer games. In a very short time, more than 100 versions of optical toys were all the rage around the world. They depicted simple action scenes. Circus clowns and acrobats were popular. So were romping dogs, capering monkeys, running horses, and swimming fish. Notwithstanding this commonplace fare, the inventors had a liking for high-falutin' labels. The gadgets bore such names as: *Fantascope, Stroboscope, Animatoscope, Filoscope,* and *Zoetrope.*

THE ZOETROPE AND MORE

The Zoetrope, invented by a man named William Horner, was one of the most popular. Perhaps this was because it permitted the viewing of any number of action scenes, each on a separate paper strip. It consisted of a drumlike metal or cardboard cylinder, open at the top and closed at the bottom by a wooden disc. This disc was mounted on a spindle, which could be held in one hand or mounted on a table, so that the cylindrical drum could be spun. A row of slotted openings was cut in the upper rim of the drum. A paper strip bearing a series of images was inserted so that it went around the inside circumference of the drum. The viewer twirled the drum and watched the succession of images through the slots as they passed before his or her eye. (To make your own Zoetrope, see Figure 28.)

By the early part of the nineteenth century, experimenters with magic lanterns and animation drawings

Fig. 10 *The Phenakistoscope copied the animation devised by ancient Greek soldiers, who drew figures on their round shields.*

were beginning to get the hang of things. In 1845 the first true movie projector was developed by Baron Franz von Uchatius. He combined the projection characteristics of the magic lantern with the slotted shutter principle of Plateau's Phenakistoscope. Thus, he made it possible to project the illusion of movement on a scale that could be seen by an audience rather than a single viewer. The baron's animation images were painted by hand on glass plates.

In spite of this step forward, almost half a century passed before anybody got around to providing a theater to capitalize on motion picture projection. A Parisian, Emile Renaud, was the first. He established his Optical Theatre in 1892, using a projector called a *Praxinoscope*, and

operated it successfully until 1900. Optical Theatre did not show true animation as we know it today. But Renaud was the first to project pictures on a large screen before an admission-paying theater audience. He used a progressive series of pictures, which were hand-drawn and were synchronized with music as an added attraction.

Meanwhile, back in the darkroom, another phenomenon was being developed: photography. It was not long before the new inventions of Daguerre, Fox Talbot, and others were being adapted for use in the magic lantern. The Langenheims of Philadelphia devised a way to make photographic glass slides, and in 1888, the Eastman Company introduced commercial celluloid film. The Lumière brothers in France were

leaders in the successful projection of pictures on film instead of glass.

Scientific, artistic, and public interest turned more and more to motion pictures using photographic images. Audiences were delighted at seeing real live people on the screen. However, the art of hand-drawn animation was far from discarded because it could depict the "impossible" antics that live action couldn't accomplish. The fact is, the development of animated films picked up speed right along with the development and widening popularity of motion pictures.

THE MODERN AGE

The year 1900 might be considered the beginning of the modern "Age of Animation." Some historians credit French animator Emile Cohl with the first authentic animated film. In truth, the honor should go to James Stewart Blackton, a comic strip cartoonist on the *New York Evening World*. Blackton dabbled with film animation on the side and actually produced two films before Cohl did. Blackton's *The Enchanted Drawing* was released in 1900, and *Humorous Phases of Funny Faces* was first shown in 1906. Cohl's first animated film, *Phantasmagorie*, appeared in 1908. To his credit, however, *Phantasmagorie* became several films and thus was the world's first animated series. Cohl also created the first animated film star, a character named Fantouche.

From there on the turnstiles were spinning. In Europe, Canada, and the United States a growing number of animators innovated and expanded the production of animated films. Russians and Germans excelled with early silhouette and cutout films, but America's cartoon animators quickly dominated the field. Most of them gravitated into films from jobs as newspaper cartoonists.

Winsor McCay, for example, put his comic strip character, Little Nemo, onto film in 1911. He made more than 4,000 drawings and, working on translucent rice paper with crossmark guides to position each drawing accurately, was able to achieve a film that was less jerky than the animation previously produced.

Some other comic strip artists who turned to animation were John R. Bray of the *Detroit Evening News*; George McManus of the *New York Journal*, best known for his characters Maggie and Jiggs; and Max Fleischer of the *Brooklyn Eagle.*

Fleischer, who launched now-famous animated features including *Out of the Inkwell, Betty Boop,* and *Popeye,* was typical of a group of dedicated artists who foresaw and participated in the growth of the animation industry. They usually were loners, seldom having contact with one another. But they were a hard lot to discourage. Fleischer worked a full year on his first animated film, which ran less than a minute. Soon, however, American and European filmgoers became accustomed to cartoon shorts with their motion pictures. In fact, they demanded them.

In an effort to meet the demand, Raoul Barre, a Canadian, established in 1913 the world's first studio devoted exclusively to the production of animated films. John Bray set up a similar studio the following year, and Pathé, a movie giant of the time, released a new Bray animated film every month.

An early female animation pioneer was Lotte Reiniger of Germany. In 1912, when she was still a teenager, Reiniger made shadow films from cutout silhouettes. In 1923, when only twenty-four years old, she made a silhouette film, *The Adventures of Prince Achmed,* which was among the earliest full-length animated films produced.

Other prominent women contributors to animation were Claire Parker of Boston and Mary Ellen Bute, a Texan. Both were innovative artists working principally in the 1930s. More recently, in England, Joy Batchelor attained prominence as co-producer of *Animal Farm,* a feature-length animated film based on George Orwell's controversial political satire.

COMMERCIALS, TOO!

Needless to say, the immense popularity of animated films and their continuing improvement in quality could not have been realized without creative experimentation. Even in the industry's infancy, when audiences were still marveling at glass-plate slides projected in modified magic lanterns, an enterprising Englishman perceived the commercial and propaganda potentials of the new medium. In 1897 Arthur Melbourne-Cooper used matchstick figures to enact the first animated commercial. It advertised Birds' Custard Powder. Two years later Melbourne-Cooper made another animated matchstick film in aid of British soldiers fighting in the Boer War.

Here are some additional interesting developments that have contributed to animation as we enjoy it today:

- In the mid-eighteenth century the Dutch scientist Musschenbroek, mentioned earlier, conceived the idea for a double projector. One stationary image, usually the background scene, was shown on a screen, while a series of drawings on glass slides was projected onto it.

- In 1905, in Spain, Segundo de Chomon made a *stop-motion* film of animated objects titled, *El Hotel Electrico (The Electric Hotel).*

- As was mentioned earlier, Winsor McCay put cartoon animators on the road to smooth, "fluid" motion by putting *register* marks on his drawings. McCay also introduced a production time — and expense — saver called the "animation cycle." This is the repeated use of an identical series of drawings to create the illusion of continuing motion. McCay relied heavily on cycles in his second and third animated films, *How a Mosquito Operates* and *Gertie, the Trained Dinosaur.*

• *Cels*, the transparent, perforated sheets used in making cartoon animation (described in Chapters 7 and 11), were introduced in 1914 by Earl Hurd in Kansas City. He received a patent the following year.

• *The War and the Dream of Momi*, a film by Giovanni Pastrone released in Italy in 1916, combined animated puppets with live-action film, thus opening another imaginative field of possibilities.

• In the 1930s Mary Ellen Bute widened the scope of animation art by animating abstract shapes in tune with symphonic music. But one of her most notable productions, *Rhythm in Light*, combined abstract drawings with ping-pong balls, cellophane, Fourth of July sparklers, and barber poles — all photographed with variable speeds and lighting.

• Somehow *Snow White and the Seven Dwarfs* (1938) got the reputation for being the first full-length animated feature film. Actually, seven animated features had been shown in movie theaters before Snow White and her pint-sized friends became box office hits. Like *Snow White*, three of the features were produced in cartoon cel animation (see Chapter 11). The first of these appeared in Argentina in 1917. It was a political satire by Frederico Valle, titled *The Apostle.*

• The making of *Yellow Submarine*, a 1968 movie starring the Beatles, brought *pixilation* into prominence. The film, by Englishman John Dunning, combined live action, cartoon animation, and pixilation. The latter is a term for photographing human beings in stop-motion to give the illusion of seemingly impossible antics.

• Though used experimentally for some years, *rotoscoping* came into its own in 1978 with the release of *The Lord of the Rings*, Ralph Bakshi's animated adaptation of Tolkien's fabulous tale. In rotoscoping, a live-action version is filmed first. Then every frame is traced and colored to create a series of animation cels. One advan-

Fig. 11 *The Zoetrope, invented in the early part of the 19th century, became a popular home entertainment device.*

tage of the method is that it permits a high degree of accuracy in the portrayal of hand-drawn motion. In addition, large numbers of moving figures can be shown at the same time, a difficult achievement in normal cartoon animation.

What is the result of all this creativity? Over the years, moviegoers have come to know and enjoy a spectacular parade of lovable and laughable animated characters. Koko the Clown, Felix the Kat, Bugs Bunny, Donald Duck, Olive Oyl, Woody Woodpecker, Superman, Wimpy, Tom and Jerry, Gerald McBoing Boing, Porky Pig, and Mr. Magoo only begin to make up a lengthy list. You may not be old enough to have seen some of the earliest, such as Koko, Felix, Betty Boop, and Colonel Heesa Liar. But these capering cartoon characters had a profound influence on what was to follow. For example, Walt Disney's earliest drawings of Mickey Mouse were remarkably similar in technique to the drawing style of Otto Messmer's Felix the Kat.

Incidentally, Mickey was the third name given to the world's most famous mouse. He first appeared in 1928 as Steamboat Willie in what was the very first animated cartoon with a sound track. It won an Academy Award. Disney then dubbed his creation Mortimer Mouse. But his wife, Lillian, suggested Mickey Mouse and that name stuck. Credit for Mickey's rounded figure should go to Ubbe Iwerks, pronounced "eye works," who was chief animator in the early days of the Disney studio. Iwerks refined many of Disney's original drawings and contributed numerous technical improvements to the art of animation.

Unfortunately, one of the most valuable creative features in the heyday of cartoon movie shorts has fallen

victim to television's voracious appetite for animation. The superb characterization and particularly the sophisticated drawings, color, and movement that marked the movie productions have been partially abandoned in the interest of rapid mass production. The result is that nearly all the cartoon animation seen on your television screen today incorporates a time-saving and cost-saving technique called *limited animation*. It is a method in cel animation (explained in Chapter 11) in which only the portion of a figure that is currently moving is redrawn again and again. The rest of the figure and scene is stationary and, as a result, tends to appear stiff and lifeless on the screen. It's a hop, skip, and jump backward to earlier, cruder days of animation.

This corner-cutting trend is counterbalanced, however, by the creative excellence of feature-length films, which have raised animation to the level of fine art. Disney really set the ball bouncing in 1932 when he introduced full color to animation in a film called *Flowers and Trees*, a forerunner of *Fantasia*. Both these films also demonstrated what could be accomplished with the creative use of background music.

The producers of animated feature-length films have never looked back. As new techniques have been developed, even greater creative flair has enraptured theater audiences. *The Lord of the Rings* brought the fine detail and animated realism of rotoscoping to the screen, and feature films like *Tron* introduced the bedazzling fantasies of computerized graphics.

The popularity of full animation as used in these films became evident at the box office in the middle of this century. Today there are well over 200 feature-length animated films available around the world.

A most recent development has been that of combining cartoon animation or object animation with live-action film, a technique borrowed from television commercials. An outstanding example of people and cartoons cavorting together is the feature-length film *Who Framed Roger Rabbit?*. In the car chase scene, for example, the action was first filmed with a real automobile, then a cartoon car and rabbit were animated and superimposed over the scene.

The movies *Star Wars* and *The Rocketeer* display the magic of object animation. In scenes of *The Rocketeer* in which the star of the film rockets across the screen, 80 percent of the action was accomplished with an animated puppet. When this movie was proposed to Disney Studios executives, they doubted it could be done. But when they were shown short segments of the rocketing puppet, the executives thought it was a live stunt man and OK'd production of the film. If you saw the movie, you probably were fooled, too.

COMPUTERS AND ANIMATION

With the arrival of computers, it was inevitable that the creative artistry of the animator and the technical know-how of computer scientists would begin a courtship, the object of which was matrimony. The nuptials have occurred, but not without some difficulty and not yet to the full satisfaction of the consenting parties. What may appear to the viewing public to be phenomenal technical and aes-

thetic advances only whets the appetite of computer animators to surmount obstacles that keep them from even greater accomplishment.

Chief among the obstacles is the enormous cost for the hardware necessary to do high quality animation. (Yes, you *can* do a type of animation similar to, say, PACMAN on a microcomputer, but the color range is limited and the resolution is poor.) Hence, to date, computer-generated animation and computer-assisted animation have been generally limited to short segments and have been done by educational and industrial institutions. They have been interested less in entertainment than in solving specific scientific problems or advancing the computer animation processes themselves. For example, one of the first computer-generated animation films, produced at Bell Laboratories in 1961, was only four minutes long and bore the tantalizing title, *Two-Gyro Gravity-Gradient Attitude Control System*.

However, traditional animators did not take long to see advantages in the use of computers for entertainment, and hang the expense. Some teamed with computer experts to develop software to assist and speed up cartoon and object animation and to provide special effects for movies. A case in point is the T-1000 Cyborg that appeared in Arnold Schwarzenegger's film *Terminator 2: Judgement Day*. Thirty-five computer animators spent ten months producing images of the cyborg, which appears only about five min-

utes on the screen. The cost: $1 million per minute! That's more than Schwarzenegger makes.

Financial requirements such as the above explain why movie producers have been slow to embrace the developing computer technologies. But attitudes are changing as more and more examples prove the efficacy of computer-generated animation. Each year more movies appear with computer-animated segments. But as yet, with one exception, no one has ventured to risk capital on a feature-length computer-animated film. The exception is one presently in the works for Disney Studios by Pixar, Inc., a technology company in California that produces both animation for TV commercials and software for computer animators. The contract for the as-yet unnamed Disney movie was signed in 1990 and will take several years to complete.

At its best, computer animation gives images the effect of being three-dimensional, something even the finest traditional drawn animation can't fully achieve. But computer animators are still unable to give their characters a lifelike aspect. They haven't the naturalness of movement that the best hand-drawn figures display. Perhaps that's why experts in the animation business say computer animation probably never will replace drawn animation, any more than animation has replaced live-action films. There's a place for all types — and movie-goers want to see them all.

3

CHOOSING
A STORY
AND
CHARACTERS

Nobody starts out to do an animated film just for the sake of doing animation. Animators do it because they have something they want to say. It may be a visual message entirely without words that someone wants to communicate to others. Animation is one of the most effective methods of non-verbal communication.

True, you could start making an animated film without a *complete* message in mind. Some fiction writers have this knack, just letting a story develop as it goes along. But, bearing in mind the considerable amount of work involved in photographing the many frames needed for even a short animated film, that's a mighty risky venture and probably a wasteful one in the bargain. You could even decide, as a beginner, to do nothing more than show some simple action without a story at all. But even if you started from scratch and made things up as you went click-click-clicking along, you would still have to decide what sort of character or object to show on the animated screen. So you see, animation has a beginning that starts considerably sooner than setting up a camera and starting to snap pictures. In fact, it has been pointed out by movie professionals that animated films require more precise preparation than do most live-action motion pictures. So go at it sensibly and carefully and consider first what you want to say.

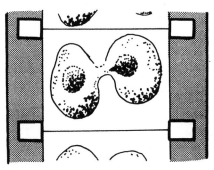

Fig. 12 *Animation is helpful in demonstrating many school subjects. Here a molecule is shown separating in a chemistry film.*

Fig. 13 *You don't have to be able to draw. This figure was snipped from an advertisement and used in cutout animation.*

CHOOSING YOUR MESSAGE

Animation is used to say a lot of things. There are movie and television entertainment, training and educational films, business and technical reports, sales presentations, and, of course, the ubiquitous TV commercial. For starters, however, you may simply want to do a short segment of fiction, a little story you make up with a touch of whimsy or one with a moral, such as an Aesop fable. If you can't think of a story of your own, why not write down a joke you heard recently, one that has some action in it, and put that onto film. (Make it a clean joke. We don't want to get involved with X-rated films right off the bat, do we?)

On a more practical note, you can use simple animation to demonstrate a concept or process for use in your job or in your club, school, and other activities. For example, show how molecules rearrange themselves in a chemical reaction, or the movement of wholesale prices in the past decade. How about giving your local football coach a hand by doing an animated diagram of a football play? If you want ideas for easy animation, go to a school and watch teachers as they diagram things on the chalkboard. The step-by-step progress of what they draw on the board will reveal a pattern for a series of animation drawings.

The decision as to what you want to say in your film will, in turn, determine whether you will need to show animated people and/or animals, moving objects, lines, numbers, abstract shapes, or combinations of them. And when *that* decision is nailed down, you will then have to decide the best way of doing the animation. Some stories are most effective when shown in cartoons. Others can be done with cutouts, puppets, animated objects, or stop-motion.

All these methods will be dealt with in detail later. The reason for bringing them up now is to impress on you that it is wise to think out the message or story you want to communicate, and how to go about it, *before* you get down to the nitty-gritty of animation production. Think about your story or message *now*, then, as different techniques are discussed and explained in subsequent chapters, you can consciously work out the details of its production.

WHAT IF YOU "CAN'T DRAW"?

At this point some people may have misgivings about their ability to draw the characters for their first animated films. An easy way to duck the problem is to choose a story line that can be peopled with cutout figures that are snipped from magazines or newspapers (Figure 13). These figures are mounted on thin cardboard and are moved about in the cutout animation technique described in Chapter 10.

Another method is to devise stories in which puppets, dolls, or simple objects can become the main characters. This is not an evasion of an art form, because such items are often used by professional animators to create sophisticated and highly successful films.

Fig. 14 *Animation art ranges from the very simple to the very complex. Develop a drawing style you can handle easily.*

For the non-artist or the beginning art student with doubts about his or her ability to draw cartoon animation, even this technique need not be a roadblock. Don't think of animation in terms of full-color scenes from *Snow White and the Seven Dwarfs*. Note, instead, some of the very simple line drawings being used in today's animated television programs for children. When starting to draw, concentrate on essentials, keep things simple, and you have every chance of success with cartoons, too.

BASIC CARTOON LESSONS

Since much material in the following chapters deals with cartoon animation and techniques related to it, this is as good a time as any to get in a few basic lessons in cartooning for animation.

First, to set your mind at ease, look at the cartoon characters in Figure 14. They were all drawn for use in cel animation, and they're recognizable as people, aren't they? Each has a head, body, two each of arms, legs, etc. Eyes, mouths, and so forth seem to check out. But they certainly don't have the same body proportions as normal human beings, do they? In fact, some of them look like simple doodles that anyone can do.

That's the nice thing about drawing cartoons for animation — you can distort, shrink, expand, and ignore the rules of anatomy all you please, and nobody will ever complain. (Did you ever notice that Mickey Mouse only has a thumb and three fingers on each hand?)

Consider a male human, for example. In real life an average man's total height is about 7 1/2 times the height of his head. In other words, we say a man is 7 1/2 heads high. (The average woman is 7 heads high.) But nobody thinks the less of Max

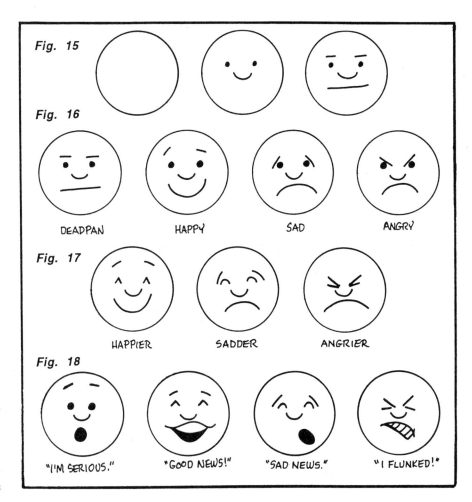

Fleischer's Popeye because the pugnacious sailor stands only four heads high and his forearms are thicker than his head. Fred Flintstone and Mr. Magoo are only three heads high. Some animated cartoon figures, like Ziggy, are little more than heads with arms and legs attached.

There's even an advantage to this. If your cartoon characters are going to have speaking roles or changing expressions, you're better off if you provide as much head space as possible for manipulating their mouths and other facial features. To give you some initial practice in this area, let's start by drawing a simple circular head and see what can be accomplished with a few lines and dots. "The fewer, the better" is a basic rule of animation.

You could make do by drawing a "Happy Face" (Figure 14), which is a circle, two dots, and a curved dash. But since the purpose here is to develop your skills, start instead by drawing a circle, two dots, and four dashes. You'll be surprised how much you can accomplish with that limited set of graphic symbols. Just follow the directions in Figure 15.

1. Draw a basic circle or oval for use as your cartoon head.

2. Put a short, slightly curved "nose" line in the center of the circle, then two dots above and slightly to the sides of the line. See, already a face is beginning to emerge.

3. Now, draw a straight horizontal line under the curved "nose" line, and two shorter horizontal

lines above the two dots. Suddenly these little lines become a mouth and two eyebrows — and you have completed a basic cartoon face. Easy, wasn't it?

Now, you're bound to ask a logical question: How do I "animate" the face to make it change expression — even talk?

That's easy. To change expressions you simply bend the mouth line up or down and move the eyebrows (Figure 16). You can show a deadpan look, a happy, sad, or angry look, always using the same number of lines and dots. Change the eye dots to little lines, just as you squint your own eyes in real life, and the expressions intensify (Figure 17).

Change the mouth line to various shapes, and your cartoon character's lips seem to be moving (Figure 18). He talks! (We'll go into this in detail later in this book.)

But you'll want to have more than one moon-faced character for the stories you want to animate. Eventually you'll want to draw characters of all types, both sexes, young and old. This means you'll be adding more details to your basic drawing. This, too, can be accomplished with a few lines; it doesn't take a great deal of art talent.

A basic rule to remember is that head shapes help tell your viewer a lot about your characters. If your planned character is to be tall and skinny, you'll need an oval-shaped head. Fat, jovial characters typically have round heads; rugged he-men have square jaws; petite lasses have dainty, pointed chins, and so on in countless variations. A lot of animated cartoon characters have no chins at all. Their heads and bodies are integrated into the least common denominators.

Another rule of animation draw-

ing, also copied from real life, is that age can be indicated by where you place the facial features in the circle of the head (Figure 19). To make the same features look as if they belong to an older person, simply move them higher on the head.

Now comes the fun part — making a whole "melting pot" of characters with a few economical strokes of the pen. It's fun because there are no set rules. All you need is observation and practice — the more practice the better. For some guides to start you doodling, see Figures 20 and 21.

Of course, the variations in types of eyes, noses, mouths, ears, hairstyles, and accessories that can be drawn are limitless. You can get a sampling of this variety, and some beneficial practice, by closely observing and copying the comic strip characters in your newspaper.

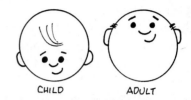

Fig. 19

CHILD   ADULT

Don't be ashamed to copy to get the hang of cartooning. As you continue to draw, your personal style will emerge, provided you draw often enough. The more you practice, the more comfortable you will be with your own distinctive drawing style. It will not only be easier for you to draw, you will be able to take liberties with your drawing and thus achieve more imaginative animation sequences.

As was mentioned earlier, the purpose of this brief cartoon lesson is primarily to show non-artists and timid ones that you, too, can draw

Fig. 20 Simply change the hair style to indicate age or sex.

GIRL   BOY   MAN   WOMAN

Fig. 21 Use hats to establish characters and occupations.

cartoons for animation. It is to be hoped that you are convinced. Some specific guidelines for drawing certain movements, backgrounds, and special effects on animation cels are covered in detail in later chapters.

DON'T OVERDO IT

On the other hand, it should be pointed out that if you are a really capable artist approaching cel and cutout animation, your skills can be your own worst enemy. The really talented person tends to draw too much and too well for animation, where the really effective talent is to know *how much* to draw. Over-elaborate drawings are difficult to redraw accurately again and again on a series of cels. The effective animator must learn to adapt his or her talents to the discipline and economy of line necessary for good animation.

This aspect of animation surfaced when the Disney studio began to develop a feature-length version of *Alice in Wonderland* some years ago. The studio artists used as their models the marvelously detailed and shaded pen-and-ink drawings done by Tenniel for the original publication of *Alice*. The animators had great difficulty resisting the temptation to include some of the fine-line techniques of the original art. This would have made the film too time-consuming and costly, so they reluctantly avoided it. Fortunately, the use of full color made up for the loss.

Perhaps the best thought an accomplished artist can carry into the design of cartoon characters for animation is that the lines *left out* of the drawing are often as important as the ones put in. A good exercise is to draw a character as you think you would want it in your film, then see if you can remove or simplify a line or two and still retain an effective character.

Remember, an animated film with sound moves at a speed of 24 frames per second. Even if you shoot each frame twice or more, a common practice in animation, you will have to draw something on the order of 720 cels just to get one minute of animation for a single character. That's why we will be talking about production shortcuts in later chapters. But even the time- and work-savers can't lessen the importance of planning and careful preparation of your visual ideas for film.

4

ANIMATION WITHOUT FILM

Anxious as you may be to start making and projecting animated films, first take a step back into history for a short session of basic training. By actually making and operating some of the "ancient" animation devices mentioned in Chapter 2, you will get a practical demonstration of persistence of vision and a better understanding of how the animation process works. You will also get a chance to put your drawing, lettering, and other practical skills to use. What's more, you'll have fun.

THAUMATROPE

Start with the easiest animation invention, the Thaumatrope (Figure 9 on page 16). Dr. John Paris, an Englishman, made the first ones back in the 1820s using a bit of cardboard and two pieces of string.

You'll need:

• A small piece of cardboard or illustration board, white on both sides.

• Two pieces of string, each about 4 inches (10cm) long.

Draw a circular disc about 2 inches (5cm) in diameter on the cardboard and cut it out. Punch small holes at the left and right sides of the disc near the edge. With pen and ink or a felt marker, letter the words I and YOU on the disc as shown in Figure 22. Turn the disc over and draw a heart in the center. Now, insert and tie the two strings in holes in the disc. (You can add a modern touch by substituting rubber bands, if you wish.)

Congratulations! You have just made a Thaumatrope as good as the one the good doctor devised. Hold the strings as shown in Figure 9 and roll them between thumbs and forefingers. The disc will whirl, and your persistence of vision will blend the lettering and heart into a single message: "I LOVE YOU."

Don't fret if you don't have a piece of cardboard that is white on

Fig. 22 *An easy-to-make Thaumatrope.*

both sides. If one side is gray, tan, or some other pale color, note the interesting color variation that results when the disc whirls. You may wish to experiment further with various color combinations on discs.

Also create some interesting visual combinations with lettering and drawings. For example, draw combinations on discs that will result in a monkey in a cage (Figure 9), a man holding a sign, a man and woman facing each other in conversation, and a seal balancing a ball on its nose. Note that you must be careful in positioning the components so that they will combine correctly when the disc is spun. This care will help you when you get into film animation.

FLIP BOOK

You have already experienced an example of flip book animation in the margins of this book. But if you make one of your own, you'll get some practice drawing and positioning material to give the illusion of movement. What's more, you will quickly learn the value of simplifying your drawings to the fewest possible lines to express what you wish to portray.

You'll need:

- A small pad of paper about 3" x 5" (7.5 x 13 cm) in size. The paper should be stiff enough to spring back into position when bent and released (Figure 23). Good quality drawing paper usually will do. Thin, limp paper such as cheap typing paper won't work.

If you can't obtain a ready-made pad with the right amount of springiness in the paper, find, instead, the right sort of paper and cut and staple it together. It may even work to your advantage, because it is easier to draw or trace a series of drawings on individual sheets of paper before stapling than on an assembled pad. You

Fig. 23 *One way to hold a flip book.*

Fig. 24

Fig. 25 *A diagram of the soldier's arm movements.*

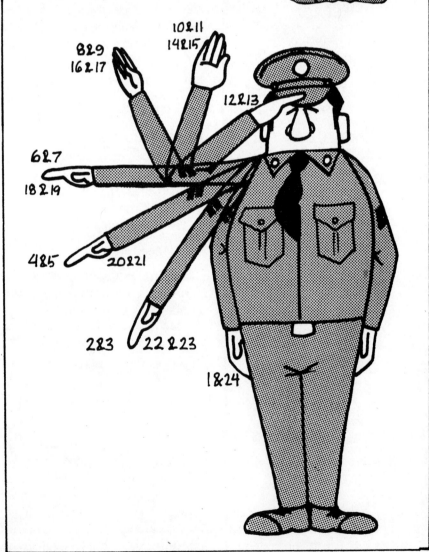

can also decide whether it is easier for you to flip the pages from front to back or back to front, as a southpaw would, and assemble your pad accordingly.

Choose a simple subject for your flip book animation — a fluttering leaf, a girl on a pogo stick, a hopping frog. Make a few trial drawings to establish a correct size and sequence before tracing them on your pad.

Start now to think habitually in one-second segments. (We're making a flip book to get to know basic animation methods, remember.) That means you think in terms of movements expressed in either 18 or 24 drawings for each second to be shown. The reason for this is that silent films are projected at a speed of 18 frames per second (*fps*) and films with sound are shown at a rate of 24 fps. Since an animated film with sound is more desirable and, we hope, your ultimate goal, plan your flip book on the basis of 24-frame sequences.

The most practical way to draw an animated movement in 24 steps is to start at the two ends and fill in the middle. Say, for example, you are to draw in your flip book a soldier saluting (Figure 24).

1. You first decide the limits of the action, that is the start and finish, and establish your *key drawings*. In this case you're in luck, because the limits of the soldier's salute are identical. He is standing at attention with his arms at his sides both before and after the saluting motion. One drawing will suffice (Figure 25) for both start and finish.

2. Next, determine where his arm and hand will be halfway through the sequence and draw them in that position. In our example, the hand is at the soldier's forehead in the salute position.

Fig. 26 *Professionals "flip" their drawings to check the effectiveness of the action they're portraying. An example of this is the "squash" at the end of this bird's flight.*

3. Now draw the position halfway between standing at attention and the full salute. As you can see, the arm is extended straight out from the shoulder in a horizontal position. This is called an *in-between* in animation parlance, because it is a drawing of a stage of the motion in between key drawings.

4. Next, draw additional in-betweens showing the intervening stages of the salute. Note that, above the level of the shoulder, only the forearm moves and the hand turns 90 degrees at the wrist.

But, hold on, you say. We were intending a sequence of 24 frames and have made only seven drawings. Somebody must have flunked math.

Not so. You've just had another lesson in the application of persistence of vision. Since the eye retains an image for a fraction of a second, you don't have to change your drawings for every frame. It is common practice when photographing animation to *double frame* or shoot *on twos*; that is, to shoot two frames on each drawing. We're doing the same in your flip book.

Your next task is to trace the seven basic drawings onto the pages of the flip book in the proper sequence, double framing as you go. The numbered sequence is shown in Figure 25, starting with the soldier at attention as Position 1. The figure is then traced with the arm at Position 2, and an identical drawing is traced on the succeeding page to represent Position 3. Repeat this for Positions 4 and 5, 6 and 7, and so on, up and back, until your soldier is at attention again in Frame 24.

You have also just been introduced to something called *limited animation*, a very common technique used in the mass production of animation cartoons for Saturday's children's shows on television. After a key drawing is established (in your case the soldier standing at attention), only the moving portion is redrawn.

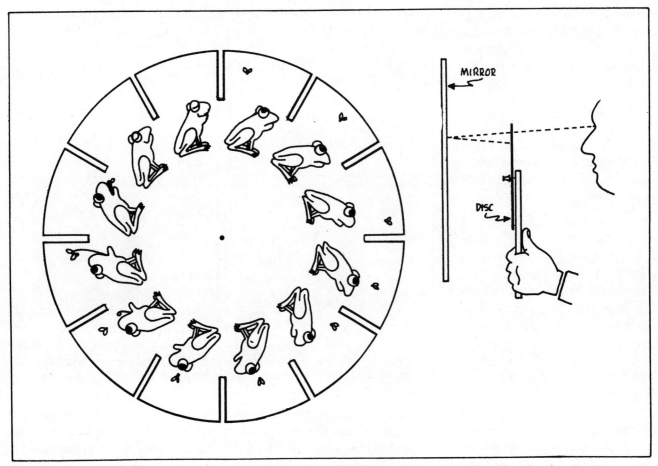

Fig. 27 *A Phenakistoscope can be made with some illustration board, a wooden stick, and a thumbtack.*

We will go into limited animation more thoroughly later on when discussing cutouts and cel animation, because it is a great timesaver. However, to make a flip book, you will have to trace or redraw the full figure of the soldier on each page.

If all this flipping business seems a bit rudimentary, don't make the mistake of discounting the importance of the flip book in the production of animation. The *flipping* technique has practical, time-saving applications, which are used as a matter of course by professionals as a quick way of visually testing proposed action sequences.

Take, for example, a flying bird (Figure 26). At the end of the flight, note how the impact is exaggerated by squashing the bird almost flat. If

an animator making a film of the bird wanted to check the effectiveness of the *squash*, he or she would hold the original drawings together like a flip book and flip them. Thus, the action can be checked before expending the time and effort painting it on cels. Later on, when you are doing your own cel animation, you'll find trial sketches viewed in flip book fashion a handy way of pre-testing your work — if not an occasional lifesaver.

PHENAKISTOSCOPE

Transfer your flip book drawings to a cardboard disc to make a simplified version of another pioneering animation device, Joseph Plateau's famous Phenakistoscope. It will provide you with a practical demonstration of persistence of vision, on which animation rests.

You'll need:

• Heavy illustration board at least 10 inches (25cm) square.

• A wooden stick about 14 inches long and 1 inch thick (25 x 25 x 2.5 cm).

• A thumbtack or pushpin.

• A mirror.

Draw a circle with a 10-inch (25cm) diameter on the illustration board. Cut out this disc. Divide the circumference of the disc into 12 equal parts and cut a slot at each point that you mark (Figure 27). The slots should be 1/4 inch (.63cm) wide and approximately 1 inch (2.5cm) deep. Draw a 12-part animated sequence around the disc. Each drawing should be immediately below one of the slots. Insert the thumbtack through the center of the disc and fasten it to the wooden handle. Turn the disc several times on its thumbtack "axle" so that it will spin easily.

Now, on with the show! Grasp the handle in one hand and hold the disc up before a mirror with the animation drawings facing toward the mirror (Figure 27). Spin the disc with your other hand and peer through the slots at the image in the mirror. The separate drawings will merge into a single one with the illusion of movement.

Experiment to find the best speed for the disc to get the clearest image. You can also strengthen the image by painting the back of the disc solid black.

ZOETROPE

If you had been a kid back before the turn of the century, you might have found this one under your Christmas tree. In addition to being the subject of much scientific study, the Zoetrope proved to be a popular toy, occupying a place in homes much as video games do today. It is a revolving drum-like cylinder with animation drawings around the inner circumference. With a little ingenuity you, too, can enjoy this bit of animated nostalgia.

You'll need:

- A smooth board or piece of plywood 9 inches (23cm) square.

- Flexible illustration board 6 inches (15cm) wide and at least 30 inches (76cm) long. This board must bend around a wooden disc.

- White drawing paper or thin Bristol board, 30 inches (76cm) long.

- Two dozen small tacks.

- Rubber cement.

- Matte black poster paint.

Optional base:

- Wooden spool (sewing).

- Smooth board about 6 inches (15cm) square or larger.

- Small-diameter dowel or bolt about 3 inches (7.6cm) long, with washer.

- Wood glue.

Draw a disc with a 9-inch (23cm) diameter on the board or plywood and cut it out. Drill a hole in the center of the disc large enough to fit over the center shaft of a record player turntable.

Cut a strip from the illustration board 6 inches (15cm) wide and long enough to go around the outer edge of the wooden disc. Allow about 1 inch (2.5cm) extra for overlapping. Mark equidistant spaces for twelve slots to be cut in this strip (Figure 28). The slots should be ½ inch (1.27cm) from one edge of the strip. Each slot should be ¼ inch (.63cm) wide and about 1 inch (2.5cm) long. Cut out the slots with a razor blade or mat-cutting knife.

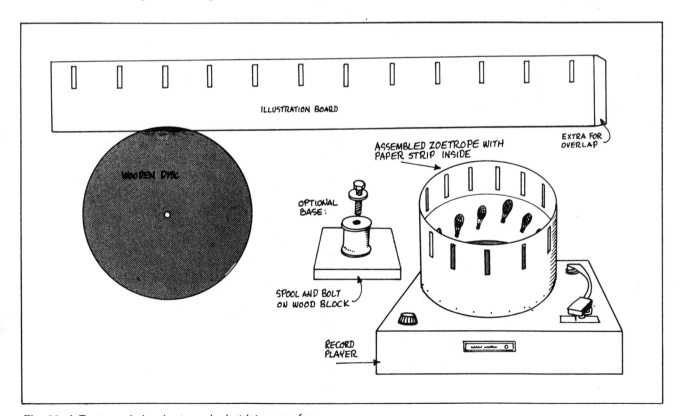

Fig. 28 *A Zoetrope is harder to make but lots more fun.*

Fig. 29 *A portion of an animated strip drawn for a Zoetrope.*

Assembling the drum:

Place the wooden disc on a flat surface and bend the illustration board strip around it, with the twelve slots nearest the top. Secure the illustration board to the disc with tacks. With rubber cement, fasten the overlapping portion of the illustration board together. You now have a firm cylinder open at the top and with a closed wooden base. Paint the outside of the cylinder black, being careful to keep paint from running through the slots to the inside.

Next, on drawing paper, mark a rectangle 3 1/2 inches (8.9cm) high and long enough to go exactly around the inner circumference of the cylinder you have assembled. Cut out the rectangle and bend it around the inside wall of the cylinder. The paper should rest on the wooden base and go up almost to the bottom of the row of slots in the cylinder wall. With a pencil, put a very faint mark on the paper just below each of the 12 slots. These marks will help you position your animation.

Remove the paper from the cylinder and draw an animation sequence on it, positioning one component at each of the pencil marks you have made (Figure 29). Put this completed "animation strip" back into the cylinder as before, making sure that each drawing is directly opposite a slot in the cylinder wall. A spot or two of rubber cement on the back of the strip will keep it in position against the cylinder.

Place your assembled Zoetrope on a record player turntable and watch the action through the slots as the cylinder revolves. The viewing principle, based on persistence of vision, is the same as that you experience while viewing animation with a Thaumatrope, flip book, or Phenakistoscope.

In case you haven't a record player handy, perhaps there is a lazy susan in the pantry that you can borrow. Or make a base for your Zoetrope with the optional materials listed earlier. Glue the spool upright in the center of the wooden board. Insert the dowel in the center hole of the spool and glue it in place with approximately 1 inch (2.5cm) extending above the spool. Center your animation cylinder on the dowel and rotate. A bit of candle wax on the top of the spool will help the cylinder spin.

This do-it-yourself Zoetrope is great for exercising your imaginative skills, because you can draw and view as many animation strips as you like. Use the gadget for experimenting—especially with animated abstract forms and color combinations. You'll find the knowledge useful in the next chapter.

5

ANIMATION WITHOUT A CAMERA

From this point on, we'll deal exclusively with the main purpose of this book — learning to produce animation *on film.*

You can actually do it without ever having to set up a camera on an animation stand or bother with light meters, focusing, and developing. You simply draw — or punch, paint, and scratch — animated images directly on blank film.

It sounds easy and it certainly can be rewarding when you see the finished product projected on a screen. But handmade films have a negative side, too, if you'll pardon the pun.

Smallness, the tiny space you have to work in, is the biggest problem. In the cel or cutout methods, animators can draw funny faces as much as 6 inches (15cm) high. But in the direct handmade technique, if you want to put the same face onto film, you'll have to squeeze it down to no more than a tiny fraction of that size. How does less than ¼ inch (6.24mm) grab you? It's great training for a steady hand in case you ever are called upon to engrave the Declaration of Independence on the head of a pin.

FILM SIZES

In order to appreciate the limitations in the size of your working area, examine the types and sizes of film stock available for direct animation.

The film strips shown in Figure 30 are actual-size drawings of 35mm, 16mm, and Super 8 film. You'll never see real film with rectangular lines on it, of course. Blank film is just that, either completely transparent or completely opaque, except for the sprocket holes, which are there to help move those boundaries if you want them to show. (The small rectangles on the drawings are sprocket holes.)

35mm — The most desirable film for direct drawing is obviously the 35mm stock, because of its larger size. Each frame is approximately ⁴/₅" x ³/₅" (21 x 15.3 mm), a size that permits some leeway in movement and some detail in the drawing. There are four sprocket holes beside each frame. A space equal to the distance between two sprocket holes separates the individual frames.

The location of the sound track on 35mm sound film is shown as a gray strip between the right-hand sprocket holes and the frame areas.

Though good to work with because of its size, the 35mm film has disadvantages in availability and cost. It is "professional" size film, and it is not always easy to locate or rent a projector for this size. It is possible to work with 35mm film, then have a photo processing lab reduce it to 16mm or 8mm size for your projector, but this is an expensive proposition, as is the cost of the original 35mm film stock.

16mm — Probably the most practical choice for handmade films because of its intermediate size and its availability, 16mm stock provides a

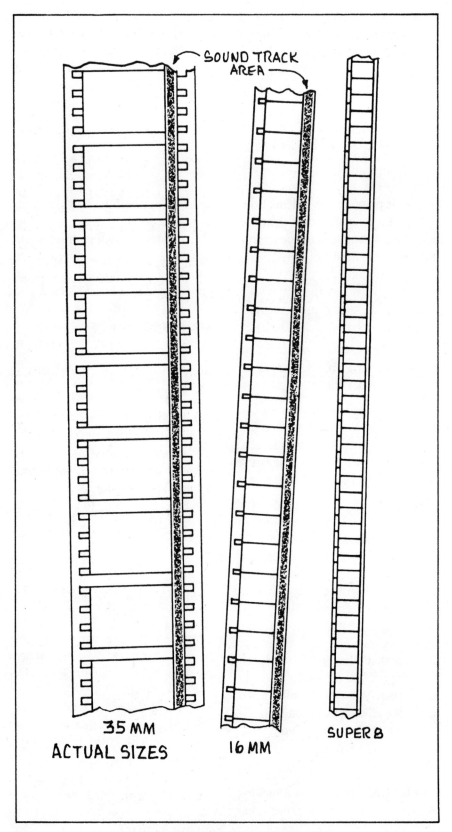

SOUND TRACK
AREA

35 MM
ACTUAL SIZES

16 MM

SUPER 8

frame area measuring about ³/₈" x ¹/₄" (9.5 x 7 mm). The actual-size drawing shown here is for sound film, and the position of the sound track is indicated by the gray strip along the right side.

This size film is also available without a sound track. The silent 16mm has a second row of sprocket holes along the right side instead of the sound track.

Note that only a thin line separates one frame from another and that the sprocket holes (only one per height of frame) are located at the separations of frames.

Sixteen millimeter projectors are used widely by schools, clubs, and serious home movie fans. They are also readily available for rent. For this reason, as well as the cheaper price of the film, the 16mm size is better than 35mm for attempting handmade films for the first time.

8mm — If you really want to think small, take a fling at working on Super 8 film — though there's precious little space for flinging. The exposure areas in the individual frames are 0.211 inch (5.39mm) wide by 0.158 inch (4.03mm) high. One sprocket hole per frame is located on the left side of the film exactly halfway up the frame. Some Super 8 film is available with a sound track. It runs along the right margin of the film.

(Though the overall widths of Super 8 and 8mm films are the same, the frame area on the Super 8 is about 20 percent larger, hence the name *Super*.)

What the Super 8 film has going for it is its cost and the fact that there are so many Super 8 projectors around. Also, despite the minuscule frame size, some very intriguing animation can be hand-drawn and scratched on the film, particularly

Fig. 30 These actual-size drawings of three strips of film show the location and areas of the "frames" that will be projected on the screen. Standard 8mm film differs from Super 8 in two ways: the frame area is slightly smaller and the sprocket holes are at the dividing lines between frames. The shaded strips on the films show the location of sound tracks.

with abstract forms and colors that run continuously through frame after frame.

OBTAINING FILM

You can purchase blank, unexposed film in camera stores, of course. Not all will have 35mm film, and some of the smaller shops will only carry 8mm and Super 8. Film processing labs usually stock all sizes of film for sale. The price of the film varies to a small degree from store to store and lab to lab, and varies considerably according to the size of the film.

Opaque film and absolutely clear film, commonly called *leader*, can also be purchased from labs and camera stores in 100-foot (30-meter) rolls. Leader is attached to the front portion of a completed film to facilitate threading the film into a projector. An additional length may also be attached at the end.

Since we want to keep your debut in film-making as economical as possible, also investigate these possibilities:

- If you are not in an animation class or working on a group project, you may still be able to obtain film at wholesale discounts. Ask the art teacher at a local high school or college about obtaining film at the special rate for schools. Or get several persons interested in film-making to pool their order in a film-buying cooperative to get the lower price on volume purchases.

- See whether local photography clubs have economical sources of film supply.

- Solicit donations of old, disused movie films from friends, schools, clubs, and other organizations. Send these to a film processing lab to have them stripped and returned to you as blank film. Better

still, strip the film yourself, using cotton swabs and bleach. Be sure to wear protective gloves.

- Though television stations are using more and more video tape, they still can be sources of discarded film, especially old, outdated commercials and promos.

- Ask your nearest film processing lab or television station for the pieces of film leader that tend to be thrown away when films are edited. Discarded leader may be in many short pieces. But it can be spliced together and, if it's FREE, it can be worth the effort. The discarded leader may be clear, opaque, or colored. This will give you a choice of experimenting with the two basic methods for working directly on film.

HAND DRAWING METHODS

Hand drawing directly on film can be accomplished with two basic methods:

1. CLEAR FILM — Pens and small brushes are used with black ink and colored inks and dyes. Felt-tipped colored markers marked "permanent" are also used extensively.

2. OPAQUE FILM—The method of drawing is to scratch away the opaque emulsion on the surface of the film, using a sharp implement or removing the emulsion with bleach.

DRAWING ON CLEAR FILM

As was mentioned previously, 16mm film is the most practical for the beginner to use for hand-drawn film making. For that reason, the explanations that follow will refer exclusively to 16mm film and the equipment needed for working with it. We will also start by drawing and painting on clear film.

MATERIALS FOR DRAWING ON CLEAR FILM

A starter kit of basic needs includes the following:

- 16mm film, preferably in a long, uncut reel to avoid the problem of splicing.

- Film-holding jig and paper templates (see Figure 31).

- Black and colored inks or dyes, with pens and small watercolor brushes.

- Colored felt-tip pens. These may be used instead of or in addition to the inks and dyes.

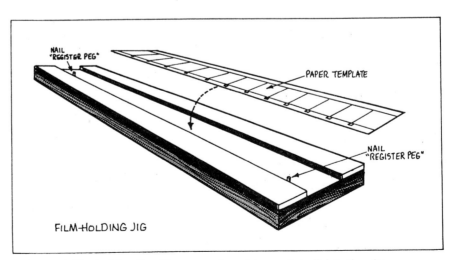

Fig. 31 *A film-holding jig with a paper template ready to fit into the slot.*

- Clean, dry rags for cleaning tools and blotting spills.
- Container of water for cleaning pens and brushes.
- A small quantity of solvent "thinner" for erasing mistakes if you are using felt pens.

Optional equipment:

- Magnifying glass.
- White cotton or nylon animator's gloves to prevent fingerprint smudges on film.

Two preparatory steps must be taken before you actually get down to the fun, as well as the hard work, of drawing directly on film.

First, you must be sure the film is ready to receive your drawings. Bleaching out the images on old, previously used film was mentioned earlier. On the other hand, if you purchase unexposed film at a camera store, you must expose it by unrolling the reel in the sunlight. Then send it to a processing lab with an explanation of what you have done and order it returned as clear, transparent film.

Second, you'll need a *film-holding jig* and some paper *templates* to guide you in the positioning of drawings on the film. The jig is a slotted gadget you can make yourself from heavy illustration board. A template is a frame-size and positioning guide drawn on a strip of paper identical to the drawing of 16mm film shown in Figure 30. You can photocopy that one. If you choose to draw your own, be sure the dimensions are the same.

MAKING A FILM-HOLDING JIG

A handy size for a jig to hold 16mm film flat and steady is 10" x 4" (approximately 25cm long and 10cm wide). The length is more than ample to accommodate 24 frames of film with some to spare. Thus, with the film held in the jig, you can work with a one-second segment of your film. The film lies in a slot and is held there by register pegs. The materials you'll need are flat four- or six-ply illustration or mat board, preferably white; a flat, smooth wooden board; glue or rubber cement; two small headless nails. Here's how it's made:

1. Cut a rectangle of illustration or mat board 10" x 4" (25 x 10 cm) and glue this firmly to a flat wooden board the same size. Weigh down the assembled pieces to ensure that the illustration board will remain flat, and allow the glue to dry.

2. Place a strip of 16mm film lengthwise on the illustration board and draw a line along both edges of the film.

3. Cut two strips of illustration board the same length, but much narrower than the first. At least one side of each of these strips should be perfectly straight.

4. Glue the strips to the larger piece, with their straight edges along the parallel lines you have drawn as a guide. The result should be a slot as deep as one thickness of illustration board and just a tiny bit wider than the 16mm film. The film should fit easily but snugly in the slot.

5. Again using a strip of 16mm film as a guide, position the film in the slot with the sprocket holes on the left side. Near each end of the jig drive a short, headless nail through a sprocket hole and into the wooden base. The film should go onto and lift off from these *register pegs* with ease.

Regarding other items on the preceding list of materials:

INKS AND DYES — Certain black inks made by Pelikan and Koh-I-Noor are suitable for drawing on cellulose film and acetate. Be sure the Pelikan ink you buy has a bold-face "T" on the label. The Koh-I-Noor black ink formulated for Rapidograph technical pens is suitable for work on film.

Today, there is a broad selection of colored inks and dyes developed specifically for animators. They were formulated primarily for use on animation cels but will do for direct drawing on film as well. (They can also be used on just about every other surface artists work on, including glass and vinyl.) Among the best of these is a group labeled *Cel-Vinyl Colors*. They combine color pigments with vinyl acrylic copolymer. They are water soluble, but dry quickly and are waterproof and smudgeproof when dry. The color selections run to forty or more.

Koh-I-Noor also makes a limited selection of colored inks for use on acetate and, therefore, film. These are specifically labeled "acetate ink."

When obtaining colors for use on clear film, remember that they should be the transparent type. Opaque colors project as solid black or brownish gray.

FELT MARKERS — Be certain that the felt-tip markers you use are the type recommended for use on acetate. These are labeled "permanent" or "permanent for projection." If not thus labeled, they will smear or rub off the film as you work with it. Worse, they can rub off and collect inside your projector.

SOLVENT — The solvent "thinner" mentioned in the materials list is the type normally used for thinning rubber cement.

You may know an art teacher who already has a good source of inks, dyes, and other animation supplies. If not, your local art supply dealer can make special orders for you.

Two good direct sources of supplies are Cartoon Color Company, Inc., 9024 Lindblade Street, Culver City, CA 90230, and Arthur Brown & Bro., Inc., 2 West 46th Street, New York, NY 10036.

USING PAPER TEMPLATES

You have an idea for an animated sequence and have assembled your materials. The next step is to plot your film on paper, pre-determining the positions of the images in the frames. It's always good practice to plan ahead, but since you will be working on blank film, you will also need a method for accurately determining the size and sequence of the frames as you draw in them. This takes us back to Figure 30 and the drawing of a strip of 16mm film.

This actual-size drawing can be traced and used as a paper template on which to draw an animated sequence before you trace it on film. You will need several such templates — enough to provide 24 frames for each second of your film. So make photocopies of your tracing. When the strips are cut from the photostat paper, they should fit snugly in the slot of your film-holding jig.

AT LAST, WE START TO DRAW!

It is imperative that the idea for your animated film requires only the simplest of drawings. When working at such a small scale, it is difficult to draw the tiny changes in movement that are needed. Also, those portions of the drawing that do not move must be in exactly the same position from frame to frame. Complex drawings are almost impossible to retrace accurately. The result is jerky or fuzzy images when projected.

You can reduce the problem of gauging the tiny changes of movement in every frame by repeating

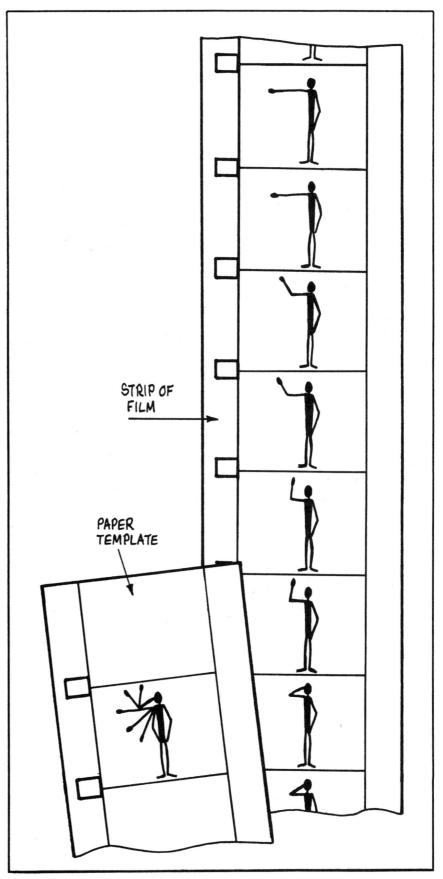

STRIP OF FILM

PAPER TEMPLATE

Fig. 32 *Enlargement of paper template showing arm positions for the saluting soldier, and the results when traced on film.*

frames. This double framing, mentioned earlier, is standard practice in professional animation because the viewer's persistence of vision permits it.

Here's a suggestion for an initial experimental film that is easy to draw. Go back to the saluting soldier you drew for the little flip book in Chapter 4. Do a stick figure version of the saluting motion shown in Figure 25 on page 30. First, draw it on one of the paper templates you have prepared; then trace the increments of movement onto your film.

Since the saluting soldier is an example of limited animation (only the arm moves), you can do the entire breakdown of movement in one frame of the template (Figure 32). After doing this, place the template in the slot of the film-holding jig with the drawn-on-frame in the first (top) position. Place your clear film over the template, securing both in position on the register pegs. Allow a little more than 6 feet (2 meters) of film to precede the first frame you will draw in. You will need this blank film as leader for threading into the projector. (You can also use this space for adding a title and credits if your film debut turns out to be runaway smash hit.)

HERE WE GO!

1. With pen and ink or fine-point felt marker, trace the stick soldier with arm in position No. 1 in frame No. 1 on your film. Use the number system in Figure 25 as a guide to the soldier's arm positions.

2. Lift the film from the pegs and move it forward one frame so that frame No. 2 is over the drawing on the paper template. Secure the film on the pegs again and retrace the soldier exactly as you did in the first frame, with his arm in position No. 1.

This is double framing.

3. Move the film forward one frame and trace the soldier with arm in position No. 2.

4. Move the film forward one frame and retrace position No. 2.

5. Move the film forward one frame and trace position No. 3.— and so on, until your soldier has completed his salute (Figure 32). You will have 26 frames of film animation. When projected on a screen, it will appear for slightly more than one second.

ONWARD MARCHING SOLDIER

Now that you're in the swing of it, so to speak, why not continue your film of the stick figure soldier to show him also turning and marching off the screen?

Plot the separate movements and draw them, frame by frame, on a paper template. Place the template in position in the film-holding jig and secure the film over it. The first frame of action following the saluting sequence should be in the top position.

This time you can trace a full 24 frames of action without lifting the film from the register pegs.

SILHOUETTES, ADD-ONS, SUBTRACTS

Now try some ideas of your own on film. At the beginning, you'll find that stick figures and solid *silhouette* figures are easier to draw and control than outline figures.

The writer recalls seeing a very funny little hand-drawn film by a high school junior in which the silhouette of a fat hen was shown pecking up dots from the ground. Each dot disappeared when pecked. The

hen grew larger and larger as she stuffed herself, eventually blanking out the entire screen.

The girl who made the film intended the dots on the ground to represent kernels of corn. But placing a succession of dots in exact position is difficult on hand-drawn films. Her dots wiggled about when the film was projected, so the film's creator wisely said they weren't kernels of corn at all; they were bugs. Smart girl.

Another easy-to-do idea is to add and subtract on film.

Start with a simple form in mind and draw only a small portion of it in the first four or six frames. Add a little more to the drawing and duplicate it for the next four or six frames. Continue in this manner until the drawing grows into a complete image. You can speed up or slow down the action by the number of frames you use for each segment. Examples of add-on and subtract animation may be seen in Figure 33.

To subtract the image, just reverse the process. Start with the full drawing and show a little less of it in succeeding groups of frames.

ABSTRACT MOTION AND COLOR

Many beginners experimenting with hand-drawn film ask:

"Why mess with all that frame counting and careful positioning? Why not draw sweeping lines that flow along the length of the film, disregarding the separations in frames?"

Fig. 33 (opposite page) Examples of hand-drawn animation on clear and opaque films. Strips A and B are examples of add-on and subtract animation. The pattern in G was achieved by punching holes in the opaque film.

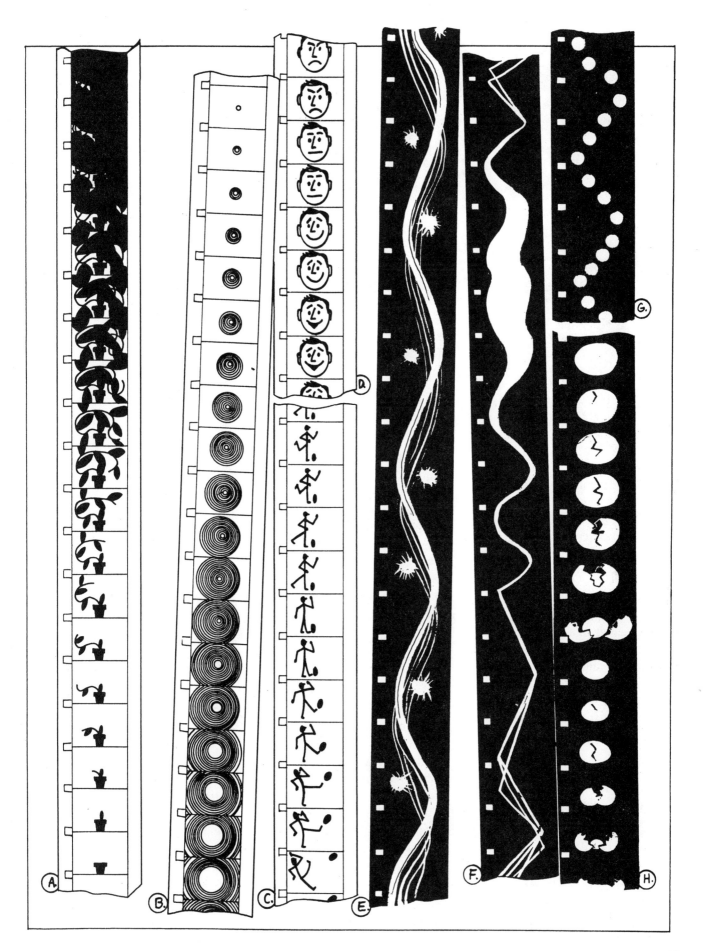

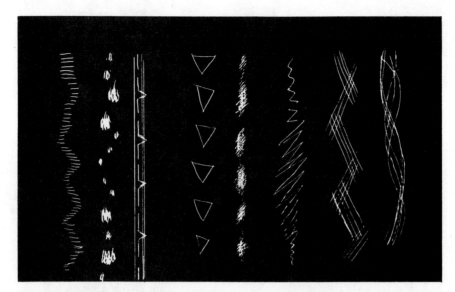

Fig. 34 *These patterns were scratched with a piece of metal window screen, a pocket knife, and a pushpin.*

Fig. 35 *(opposite page) Sturdy paper or Bristol board can be used to make a handy frame-counting jig for opaque film.*

Why not, indeed. The interplay of line and color applied at random along the clear film can result in intriguing abstract designs, "paintings in motion." The effect is further enhanced by combining opaque inks (which project as black) with transparent colors. What's more, the potential for creative variations is limitless — undulations, thick-and-thin lines, zigzags, processions of dots and blobs, forms that grow and recede.

As a matter of fact, the ordered chaos of abstract films adds to the excitement. A methodical parade of similar shapes at consistent speed is likely to be boring. So do try some abstract fun on film. Spice your drawings with irregular combinations of quick and slow movement, altered colors, and abrupt changes of light and shade. In effect, give your film a "harmony" just as if you were composing a piece of music.

One thing you'll learn from this is that, even in what appear to be the most haphazard of films, there often is methodical planning. You will probably produce better abstract films if you plot them first on paper templates before putting pen and brush to the clear film.

Consider also the matter of color harmony. Your persistence of vision retains color as well as form. Colors seen on the movie screen are strongly influenced by the colors seen in the frames immediately preceding them. Art students will find making hand-drawn films an exciting and effective way to learn how to use various color combinations.

DRAWING ON OPAQUE FILM

The creative use of abstract line and form — even color — finds an agreeable medium in opaque film. Since the solid layer of emulsion on the film makes it even more difficult to separate one frame from another than is the case with clear film, the opaque film invites the free use of lines, dots, and forms that ignore the dividing lines between frames. It is also fascinating to work figuratively in the dark and see the finished results in bright light and animated movement on the screen.

DRAWING MATERIALS FOR OPAQUE FILM

Basic needs include the following:

- Lengths of opaque black leader or fogged color film.

- Scratching and scraping tools.

- Small bottle of household bleach.

- Several cotton swabs.

- Colored permanent felt markers or transparent colored ink with brushes.

- Quantity of clean rags or absorbent cotton.

- Film-holding jig.

In case of accidental bleach spills, also have handy some vinegar to neutralize the bleach and a large bottle or pan of water.

Caution: Since this method of hand-drawing requires that you work with film coated with emulsion, be sure to specify this if buying opaque leader from a camera store or processing lab. Some stores and labs also sell solid color plastic leaders. The color is all the way through the leader and will not react fully to bleach.

SCRATCHING AND SCRAPING

Almost any sharp-pointed or sharp-edged implement can be used as a tool for making images on opaque film. By far the most commonly used are the ordinary objects at hand, such as large needles, straightened safety pins, single-edge razor blades, small scissors, pocket knives, and X-Acto

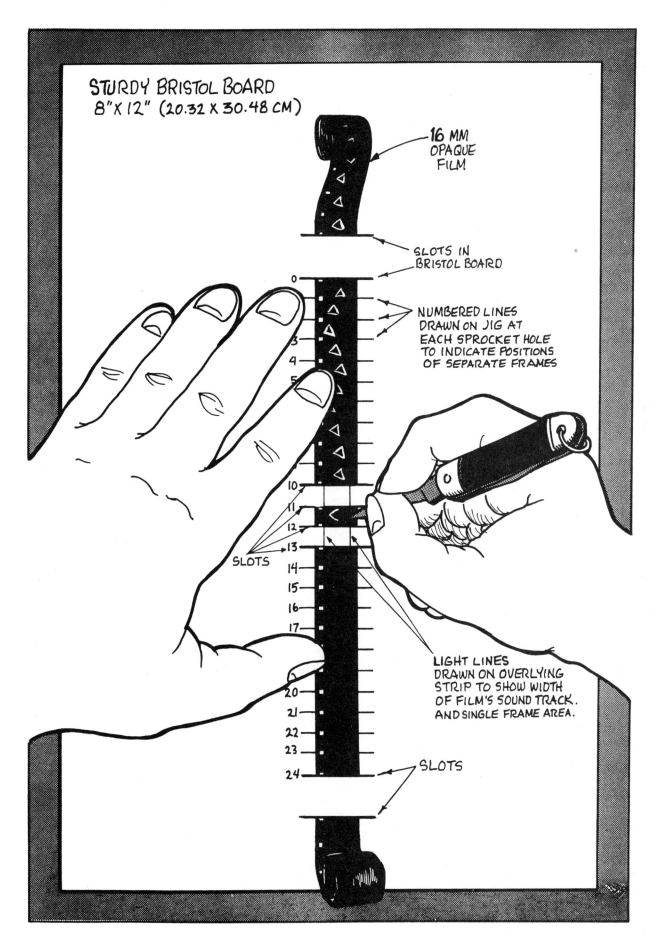

STURDY BRISTOL BOARD
8" X 12" (20.32 X 30.48 CM)

16 MM
OPAQUE
FILM

SLOTS IN
BRISTOL BOARD

NUMBERED LINES
DRAWN ON JIG AT
EACH SPROCKET HOLE
TO INDICATE POSITIONS
OF SEPARATE FRAMES

SLOTS

LIGHT LINES
DRAWN ON OVERLYING
STRIP TO SHOW WIDTH
OF FILM'S SOUND TRACK.
AND SINGLE FRAME AREA.

SLOTS

blades. Sandpaper, in any or all of its various degrees of coarseness, can also be used to obtain interesting visual effects. The edge of a small piece of window screen will make a series of parallel lines when drawn across the film emulsion. Figure 34 shows some possibilities. Try them all and find the one(s) you most enjoy working with.

STARTING FROM SCRATCH

A unique feature of hand-drawing on opaque film is that you work like an etcher or an artist drawing on scratchboard. In your case, you will be "etching" in *emulsion*, a gelatinous substance, which has been thinly applied on one side of a strip of transparent cellulose film. You scratch, scrape, and bleach away solid areas of emulsion to make images

that are transparent lines and forms. Through these, light can be projected on the screen. Hence, you must visualize in reverse. The lines you scratch in the emulsion will project as white lines in a dark area.

You must, of course, always work on the film with the emulsion (dull) side up. The fact that it is the dull side usually makes it easy to determine which is the emulsion side of the film. But if in doubt you can make these simple tests:

- When touched with a damp finger, the emulsion side will feel slightly sticky; the other side won't.

- A drop of bleach on the emulsion side will cause small bubbles to appear, and the area can be wiped clean to expose the transparent film beneath. If it fails to bubble, turn the film over and test again.

CREATING IMAGES

With the exception of the tools you use, the method of working on opaque film is much the same as the free-wheeling drawings mentioned in an earlier section about making abstract forms and color on clear film. You can scratch and scrape to your heart's content along the length of the film. You can also dip a cotton swab in bleach and draw wide lines or make dots on the film with that. Blotting the bleach off the film will provide sharper edges to the lines and forms. But also try wiping the bleach off and observe the interesting results.

What we have described so far will provide a black-and-white film when projected on a screen. But you can easily turn it into a multi-colored extravaganza by applying transparent colored inks or felt markers to all or some of the scratched-out and bleached-out areas on the film. Try it.

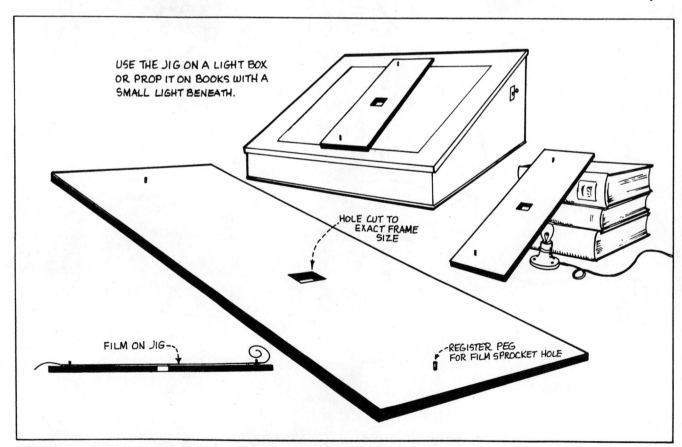

Fig. 36 A simple backlighted jig, with suggestions for lighting it.

8MM FILM, TOO

Since the abstract approach to hand-drawn film-making doesn't limit you to frame areas or require that you draw tiny images over and over, you can use this method on 8mm film with some success.

START PUNCHING

Still another method of working creatively with opaque film is to use a paper punch and perforate the film with rhythmic patterns of holes. It's easy enough to obtain an office punch that makes round holes. Perhaps you'll be lucky and locate punches that make patterned holes like those used by railroad conductors.

Try to avoid letting your punched holes extend beyond the sides of the frame areas on the film. Especially avoid the sprocket holes. The ragged edges will curl and cause the film to jam or tear in the projector. If the film has a space for a sound track, keep out of that too. It'll be useful later on if you decide to add sounds.

Incidentally, punched films do, after all, provide creative possibilities for using the solid-color plastic leaders you were cautioned against earlier.

USING A FILM-HOLDING JIG

Just as a holding jig is used to control the drawings on clear film, film holders can also serve as handy aids for working with opaque film. There are two basic types of jigs for opaque work, both easily constructed. The easiest is a *frame-counting jig*. The other is called a *backlighted jig*.

FRAME-COUNTING JIG

The frame-counting jig is merely a white rectangle of sturdy illustration or mat board. It has slots to hold down the film, and it provides a quick, visual method of checking the numbers of the frames in which you draw. Figure 35 shows a frame-counting jig in use, along with details of how it is made. The one shown is 8" x 12" (20.32 x 30.48 cm), which is long enough for you to see and work with 24 frames of 16mm film — or one second of projection time.

Start by placing a strip of film along the center of the board. Put pencil dots in the sprocket holes that mark the separations between frames. Then, draw horizontal ink lines through the dots and number them 1 through 24 from top to bottom. Note in the illustration that the lines extend beyond the sides of the opaque film when it is placed over them. Cut eight slots in the board where indicated.

By threading your film through the slots, as shown, you can hold it firmly in the jig, at the same time providing a good working surface that will catch stray splatters of bleach and coloring materials that you may use. The numbered lines will indicate the positions of individual frames and aid in developing a controlled rhythm in your patterned images.

Obviously, the lines and numbers should be made with India ink that is impervious to bleach. You can draw them directly on the board as explained above. Or draw them on thin paper and glue them in position. The latter course may become necessary if the original lines become smudged.

BACKLIGHTED JIG

If you have courage enough to attempt scratching a frame-by-frame animated sequence on opaque film, you'll need another type of film-holding arrangement. There will be no need for paper templates. You couldn't see them through the opaque film. But you can make a simple jig that will ensure that you draw within the correct frame areas. Further, the frame you draw in will be back-lighted to assist you in seeing the lines as they are scratched in the opaque emulsion.

The jig consists of a thin wooden board or piece of plywood about 6 inches (15cm) wide and twice that in length (Figure 36).

Here's how to make it:

1. In the center of the board, cut a rectangle the same dimensions as one frame area on 16mm film.

2. Position a strip of film over this "window" with two sprocket holes at its two left-hand corners.

3. Drive a register peg (short headless nail) through the film sprocket holes near each end of the board.

Place this jig on a light box, or prop it on books with a low wattage light bulb underneath, so that the light shines up through the "window." Fasten your film over the register pegs, and you're ready to scratch the first image in the frame over the lighted rectangle. When finished, lift the film from the register pegs and move it forward one space so that the next sprocket hole will fit over each peg. The device will assure correct positioning of each succeeding frame even though you haven't any paper template or guidelines to refer to.

Needless to say, your drawing must be of the simplest possible forms and images. You will not even have the luxury of tracing them.

Before projecting the film, inspect it closely and remove any tag ends, chips, or tiny shavings that may be hanging loose as a result of your scratching and scraping the emulsion. This should be done for all scratched films, because the loose ends can dislodge in the projector and will appear as great dirty blobs on the screen.

6
STOP-
MOTION

A popular form of pseudo-animation, also fun to work with, is one that had its origins back in those pioneering days when Emile Renaud was packing them in at his Optical Theatre in Paris. This is the technique of stop-motion. It is often referred to as *kinestasis*, which is easily explained by the roots of the word: *kine* (moving) and *stasis* (stillness). Stop-motion does just that. It achieves the illusion of motion out of still pictures.

Actually, the basic single-frame method used in photographing almost all animation is, in itself, stop-motion. But the term as we deal with it in this chapter means using the single-frame method to record magazine and newspaper pictures, photographs, slides, sketches, and other two-dimensional graphics. A series of these still pictures is filmed, rather than one gradually changing picture or object. The intent is to present many pictures in a short span of time to tell a story. Single pictures are seldom altered or moved. The "animation" is achieved in a rhythm resulting from the selection and fast-paced projection of the pictures. The animator often may use selected close-ups of portions of a picture as well as its entire area.

A marvelous example of this is a stop-motion documentary film with musical background that appears occasionally on television. It presents a condensed history of the United States, from early discoveries until after World War II, all in the span of about three minutes.

It's a fascinating film, even when seen several times. The country's history takes on chronological clarity as important American leaders and events flash before your eyes. The pace of the film, though rapid, alternately slows then hastens onward, depending on the events in view. The changing tempo and volume of the music reinforce the mood as excitement builds and ebbs.

You needn't take on anything as ambitious as the history of the nation to test your skill at making a stop-motion film. This technique is especially suited for making short documentaries and training films as well as comic films just for fun.

STOP-MOTION SUBJECTS

There are numerous stop-motion subjects that lend themselves to filming right in your home and backyard. Choose one and photograph it thoroughly with a still camera. Shoot from all angles and at several distances as if you were zooming in or out. Then select the best of the prints that make a sequence and transfer them to movie film by shooting them in an animation stand, using single-frame action.

An example of this is in your garden, where a series of time-lapse photographs can be made of the growth and blossoming of a plant.

On the lighter side, consider doing still photographs of a "typical" day in the life of your Aunt Mabel and putting them into a stop-motion film. Shoot long and medium shots and close-ups. Remember that the tempo of your film can be varied to express moments of excitement, boredom, gaiety, etc., during the day.

A second way of obtaining stop-motion material is to film subjects that have already been thoroughly recorded in photographs, drawings, and printed pictures in books and periodicals.

For example, gather all the pictures you can find of Leonardo da Vinci, his art and inventions, and put them together in a short film. Or do a stop-motion documentary on the works of a well-known local artist. Or, as a treat for your family, collect all the photos of a relative from infancy through adulthood and put his or her life story on film. Ask your aunt how she'd like to be in pictures.

MUSIC AND VOICE-OVER

You may wish to start out in stop-motion by making a silent film. It's simple, and you need to shoot only 18 frames for each second of projection time.

But as you gain experience and skill, you are almost certain to want to add background music, sound effects, and perhaps a voice-over commentary to your subsequent films. Even without oral commentaries, the *audio* additions of music and other sounds help your audience to capture the mood and better comprehend the message you are projecting.

The wedding of these audio elements with the visual part of the film will be discussed in Chapter 15. But it is wise to consider music briefly now in relation to stop-motion filming, because the selection and use of pictures affects the selection and use of music — and vice versa. It takes some experimentation and perhaps a knack.

The point is, you should have some sort of musical theme in mind as you make your picture selection and plot the timing of each picture's expo-sure. It is not sufficient merely to shoot an interesting array of pictures and then dub in a nice bit of music. The number of frames exposed for each picture determines the time it appears on the screen; and, ideally, the change from one picture to another should coincide with the music's beat.

As an exercise, obtain from your library or your school's music department a recording of Pachelbel's Canon No. 9. A canon is a 16th century form of musical composition with a four-beat rhythm repeated over and over. Thus, knowing the beat in advance, you can easily plot the times to change your stop-motion pictures — giving them a fast tempo or slow and easy tempo according to your need.

VISUAL RHYTHM

Always keep in mind that the visual element is the most important element of your film. Its clarity and

Fig. 37 *Three of several photos used in a brief stop-motion film entitled* Les Oiseaux à Gaspé. *The animator used close-ups of various areas in each photo. Thus, a single picture's usefulness could be extended and the film presentation made more interesting.*

48

Fig. 38 *Three of eight steel engravings used in the film* En Garde.

impact depend on your selection of pictures and the skill with which you arrange them in sequential order. Next to this in importance comes the rhythmic movement you establish with their exposure.

Effective visual rhythm in stop-motion films seldom results from a smooth, evenly-paced showing of similarly scaled pictures. That's boring rhythm. Excitement and memorability are born in varied bursts of speed with rapidly flashing patterns of pictures, sudden halts and the holding of one frame for a second or two, abrupt changes from long shots to extreme close-ups, in-and-out zooms of a single scene — and more.

HOW MANY PICTURES?

People usually have the impression that hundreds of pictures are needed to make a stop-motion film. They think a single picture is seldom, if ever, repeated. That isn't so, of course. An entire stop-motion film of several minutes' duration can be made with a mere handful of creatively manipulated pictures.

EN GARDE --- Exposure Sheet

Picture Number	Seconds on Screen	Number of Frames	Cummulative Time in Seconds	Sound Effects
1R(LS)	2	48	2	
1L "	2	48	4	
8R "	2	48	6	
8L "	2	48	8	
4L "	1	24	9	
4L(MS)	1	24	10	
5R(MS)	2	48	12	
3R(LS)	1	24	13	
7R "	1	24	14	
4L "	1	24	15	
2R "	1	24	16	
2L "	1/2	12	16.5	
2R "	1/2	12	17	
2R "	1/2	12	17.5	
5R(MS)	1/2	12	18	
4L(MS)	1	24	19	
5R(MS)	1/2	12	19.5	
3R(LS)	1/2	12	20	
2L "	1/2	12	20.5	
7R "	1/2	12	21	
2L "	1/2	12	21.5	
7R "	1/2	12	22	
2L(MS)	1	24	23	
3R(MS)	1/2	12	23.5	
2L(MS)	1/2	12	24	
3R(MS)	1/2	12	24.5	
7L(LS)	1/2	12	25	
7R "	1	24	26	Loud Breathing
7L "	1/4	6	26.25	
7R "	1/4	6	26.5	
7L "	1/4	6	26.75	Grunt
7R "	1/4	6	27	
7L "	1/4	6	27.25	
7R "	1/4	6	27.5	Grunt
7L "	1/4	6	27.75	
7R "	1/4	6	28	
6L(MS)	2	48	30	Loud Breathing
7R(CU)	2	48	32	Loud Breathing
6L(LS)	1/2	12	32.5	
6R "	1/2	12	33	
6L "	1/2	12	33.5	
6R "	1/2	12	34	
	1/2	12		

Fig. 39 *The exposure sheet for the first 34 seconds of* En Garde. *Note how the tempo of the action is varied by the number of exposures made of each picture.*

49

For example, only eight pictures were used for a three-minute film titled *En Garde*. (Three of them are shown in Figure 38.) The pictures are old engravings found in a book about dueling. The film could have been made with fewer than eight pictures, because the dueling poses are quite similar in several instances. But the film maker chose to use them all and further extended his selection with a trick you should try yourself. After photographing the eight engravings in the book and making prints, he turned the negatives over and made prints of the duelists facing in opposite directions. Thus, there were sixteen different photographs of the old engravings to work with.

En Garde is an example of utilizing changing tempos in stop-motion films. The duel opens on a slow, even beat as the opponents go through the motions of saluting each other (a courtesy traditionally accorded by persons about to skewer someone in the brisket). Quick-paced back-and-forth exposures of the two duelists give the illusion that they have touched swords and the duel is begun. The pace steadies as each feels out his adversary, then picks up speed as they feint and jab in earnest. The pace becomes so frenzied (only a quarter of a second for each facing pose) that the viewer's persistence of vision conveniently provides the illusion of a furious, sword-slashing melee. The background music builds to a frenzied pitch.

With jarring suddenness the fight stops. The music is silent. Two full-second views of the duelists show them facing each other, swords at the ready. Only the sound of heavy breathing is heard.

Just as suddenly, the fight resumes, as furious as before. Again it stops abruptly and the opponents catch their breath. The sequence is repeated until, eventually, one swordsman falls. The "victor," breathing heavily, salutes the downed man with his sword; then he, too, falls forward with a thud. Music up and out, as they say in Hollywood.

Figure 39 shows a portion of the exposure sheet worked out in advance for *En Garde*. It covers the first 34 seconds and was used by the cameraman to count frames and regulate the changes in pictures as well as the pace of the film.

You will probably enjoy the imaginative possibilities in stop-motion filming. It's an excellent technique for those who are weak at drawing. Another technique for those who don't yet feel capable of tackling the art of cel animation is three-dimensional or object animation. We'll go into that in Chapter 9.

The easiest and most practical way to manage the photography needed for a stop-motion film is to mount your movie camera (with a single-frame action) in a darkroom enlarger or on a simple animation stand that you can make yourself. Animation stands are described in the next chapter.

7

MATERIALS
AND
EQUIPMENT

By now, you are probably beginning to suspect that film animation isn't as easy to do as it appears to be on the screen.

You're right. Animation can be tough and tedious, complicated and expensive. On the other hand, animation can be a creative delight, easily accomplished with a minimal amount of equipment.

The choice is yours, depending on your interest and goals in this field.

You can actually create an imaginative animated film without using a camera. Simply scratch or paint images on blank film, as described in Chapter 5. You can produce an entertaining, technically acceptable film by placing a camera on a tripod at a sun-lit window and moving some objects about on the window sill (Chapter 9). Or you can focus a camera on a sketch pad and capture the development of a drawing as it grows, line by line. In each case, the secret of the film's success will be the idea that you film, not the sophistication or versatility of your equipment.

Nevertheless, the more your equipment can accomplish, the greater the potential of the things you can do on film and the better their quality will be. A good story idea can be helped immensely by professional touches. What's more, everything your equipment can do in accomplishing the animation means fewer repetitive and tedious chores left for you to do.

Of course, you may not plan to do all the types of animation available to you. But since the techniques are interdependent and the equipment usually identical, we will discuss in this chapter the basic equipment and materials you will need for animation in general. The specific requirements of individual animation techniques will be taken up as we come to them in later chapters. If you have already had some experience with motion picture equipment, you can, for this chapter at least, go to the head of the class.

VERTICAL AND HORIZONTAL SETUPS

What do we mean by basic equipment? There are two fundamental setups for animation, depending on the type you want to do. But with a little ingenuity, you can use either setup to accomplish the whole range of animation methods.

The most commonly used setup, a vertical arrangement, is one in which the camera is aimed downward at artwork lying on a flat surface. The basic equipment consists of the following items:

- A *baseboard* (plywood panel, drawing board, tabletop, etc.) to which material to be photographed can be fastened.

- A movie camera with single-frame action, mounted directly above the baseboard.

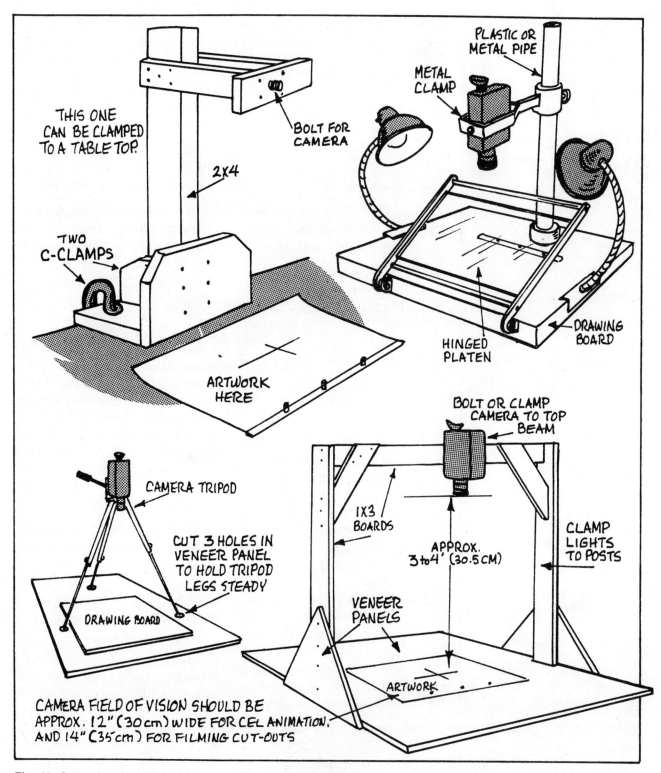

THIS ONE CAN BE CLAMPED TO A TABLE TOP.

2X4

BOLT FOR CAMERA

TWO C-CLAMPS

ARTWORK HERE

PLASTIC OR METAL PIPE

METAL CLAMP

HINGED PLATEN

DRAWING BOARD

CAMERA TRIPOD

CUT 3 HOLES IN VENEER PANEL TO HOLD TRIPOD LEGS STEADY

DRAWING BOARD

BOLT OR CLAMP CAMERA TO TOP BEAM

1X3 BOARDS

APPROX. 3 to 4' (30.5 CM)

CLAMP LIGHTS TO POSTS

VENEER PANELS

ARTWORK

CAMERA FIELD OF VISION SHOULD BE APPROX. 12" (30 cm) WIDE FOR CEL ANIMATION, AND 14" (35 cm) FOR FILMING CUT-OUTS

Fig. 40 Some suggestions for do-it-yourself animation stands.

- Two photoflood lamps, or equivalent, mounted above and on each side of the baseboard.

With these few items, you can make do very nicely, producing animation with cartoons on paper or cels, with paper cutouts, and with photos and drawings used in the stop-motion technique. Note that the materials to be photographed are all two-dimensional, flat artwork.

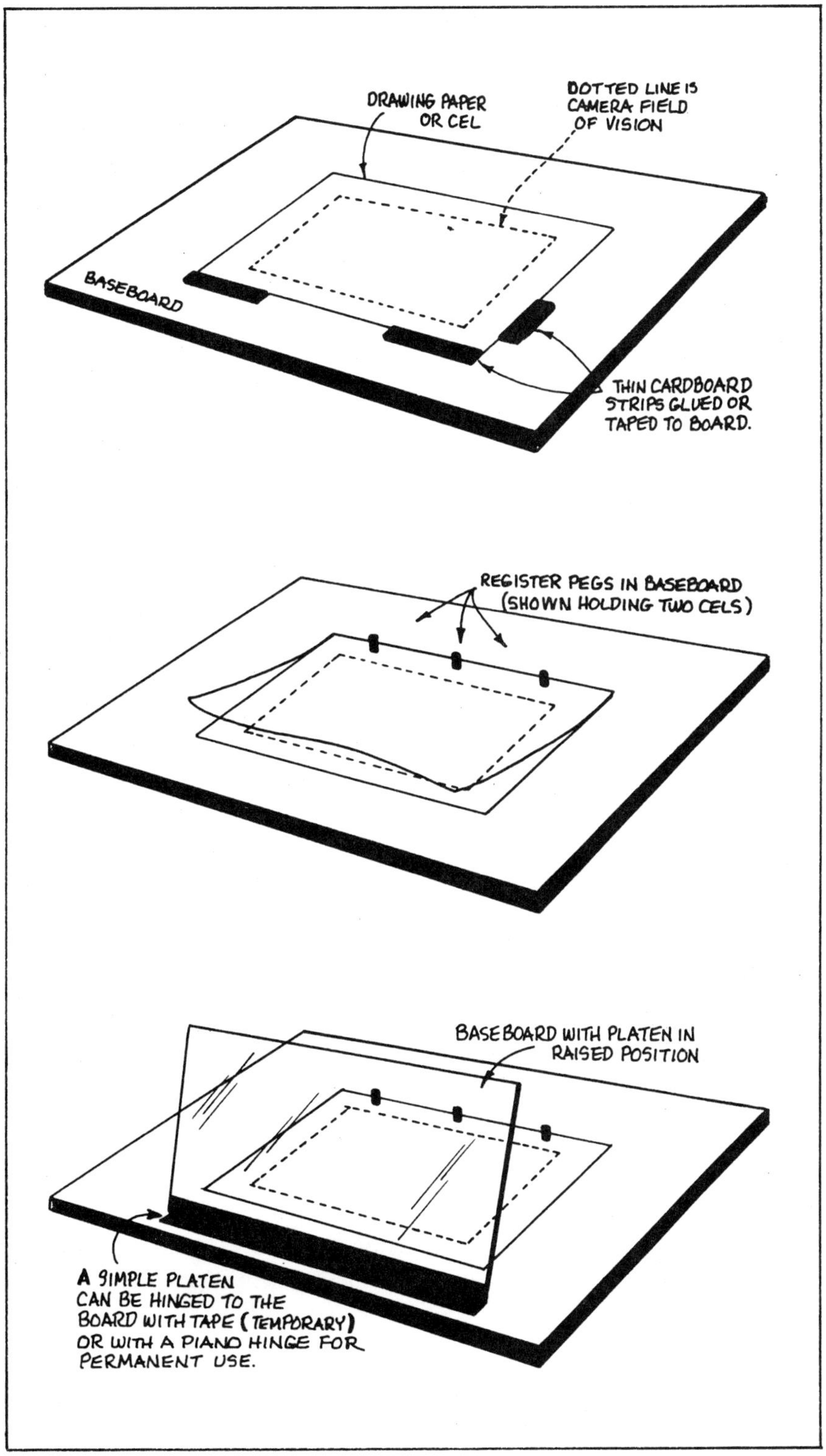

Some types of three-dimensional animation using dolls, puppets, and other objects can also be done on the setup above. For these, however, you would be better off working on a *horizontal* setup with the following basic equipment:

- A broad shelf or tabletop with a backdrop (a curtain, sheet of Bristol board, clean wall, etc.).

- A movie camera with single-frame action on a tripod or other mounting aimed horizontally at the shelf/tabletop.

- Two photoflood lamps, or equivalent, mounted above and to each side of the shelf tabletop.

A clear sheet of glass or plexiglass, called a platen, is a helpful refinement, especially when you are shooting in a vertical setup. It serves as a pressure plate to hold down drawings, cels, cutouts, and other artwork to keep them in position and to prevent disturbing shadows around the lines of cartoons and along the edges of cutouts.

If you can hinge a platen to your backdrop, flat artwork can also be filmed in a horizontal setup.

THE ANIMATION STAND

The basic equipment described above — camera, lights, working surface, and platen — is usually assembled in some sort of framework made of wood or piping. The main purpose is to hold the camera in a firm position and to help control the positioning of the material being photographed. This assembled construction is called the *animation stand*. It is the nerve center and the heart, if not the soul, of the animation process.

It is of the utmost importance to the successful animator, beginners included, to build, buy, borrow, or otherwise obtain a workable animation stand. Since the stand holds the

Fig. 41 Ways to hold artwork in position on the baseboard.

Labels in figure:
DRAWING PAPER OR CEL
DOTTED LINE IS CAMERA FIELD OF VISION
BASEBOARD
THIN CARDBOARD STRIPS GLUED OR TAPED TO BOARD.
REGISTER PEGS IN BASEBOARD (SHOWN HOLDING TWO CELS)
BASEBOARD WITH PLATEN IN RAISED POSITION
A SIMPLE PLATEN CAN BE HINGED TO THE BOARD WITH TAPE (TEMPORARY) OR WITH A PIANO HINGE FOR PERMANENT USE.

camera and the material to be photographed in absolute and unwavering position, it prevents jerky and fuzzy movements in the resulting film. The slightest inaccuracy during the photographing stage is greatly magnified on the screen when the film is projected.

But animation stands in general do far more than hold things steady. Depending on the variety of refinements built into them, versatile stands can zoom in on and away from artwork; pan, that is move the line of sight from side to side and up and down; tilt the image in the camera's eye, and more. Without such mechanical talents under his or her control, the animator needs many additional drawings or other pieces of artwork to accomplish the same action.

Commercially sold animation stands range from highly elaborate computer-controlled devices costing more than $100,000 down to small tabletop units designed for the Super 8 camera and used by students and semi-professionals. The latter units are relatively inexpensive, provided a few hundred dollars doesn't loom too menacingly in your budget.

Little wonder then, that beginners in animation want to build their own stands. Actually, it's a good idea because you can build a sturdy, workable animation stand at little cost; and, as your talents and skills develop you can add to and expand the stand's capabilities. In Figure 40 you will find some sketches of a selection of do-it-yourself animation stands in both metal and wood. Use the suggestion you can most easily construct, possibly improvising some improvements of your own.

These suggestions are for the simplest forms of animation stands. They are good starter kits to get you into the act. However, more serious ani-

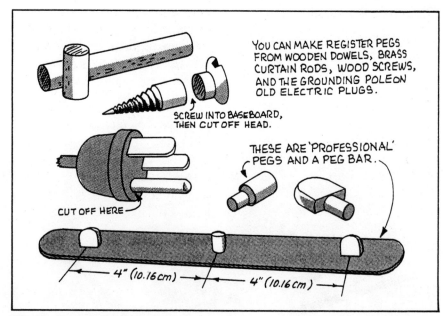

Fig. 42 *Register pegs you can make or buy.*

mators (clubs or classes) who can spend something on the order of $250 or more may wish to investigate the detailed construction plans published by Eastman Kodak Company for a marvelously versatile do-it-yourself animation stand. The exceptionally clear step-by-step instructions for the stand, which will accommodate both 16mm and Super 8 cameras, are included in a paperbound book titled *The World of Animation.* The profusely illustrated book is a pleasure to read, even if you don't plan to build an animation stand.

If you make your own animation stand and can provide an easy way to move the camera up and down, you will find this adjustable feature very handy at times. In any event, and depending on the camera you use, it should be located in an area ranging from 2 to 4 feet (0.6 to 1.2 meters) above the baseboard for convenience in working with flat artwork.

The height of the camera above the baseboard determines the camera's field of vision. Keep this in mind when planning your animation stand.

For example, if you want to do

cutout animation, a workable field of vision is 14" x 10" (35.5 x 25.4 cm). Everything you put on the baseboard should be within those dimensions, or they will be cropped out of the photo frame. Cartoon cel animation, on the other hand, can be done nicely in a field as small as 8" x 6" (20.3 x 15.2 cm). Professional cels and animation paper are generally available in 10 ½" x 12 ½" (26.7 x 31.7 cm) sheets, but at the outset you may find it more convenient and economical to obtain standard 8 ½" x 11" (21.6 x 28 cm) paper stock and clear acetate sheets at stationery and art supply stores.

Your animation stand should be designed to accommodate the largest field of vision you might possibly use, and the baseboard should be large enough to provide a means for holding flat artwork in *register* (meaning in exactly the correct position) with the fastenings outside the camera's field of vision, plus a reasonable working area around your artwork and cutouts. A baseboard measuring a little under 2 feet square (60 x 60 cm) provides a very comfortable and convenient working arrangement for 8mm animation.

REGISTER PEGS

Take a moment to consider the means for registering artwork mentioned in the previous paragraph. More than a moment, because this is a subject of utmost important to the animator. To *register* means to assure that flat artwork is positioned in exactly the correct position for each frame. Even the animator working with three-dimensional subjects will need to register artwork from time to time when filming titles, credits, and other adjuncts to a complete film.

An easy and reasonably safe way to register animation artwork is to position the first drawing correctly on the baseboard, then glue or tape strips of thin Bristol board along the bottom and one side of it. Then, assuming all of the drawings are the same size, you butt each succeeding sheet into position against the strips (Figure 41).

A better and the accepted way to register artwork for animation is with *register pegs*. The basic idea is simple. You mount two or three small pegs in a drawing board and similar ones in the baseboard of the animation stand. You punch corresponding holes in each sheet of drawing paper, photograph, or cel that you use, and you fit them over the pegs when preparing artwork and when photographing it (Figure 41). Thus, each succeeding piece is in exactly the same position as the preceding ones and any that will follow.

One rather drastic but effective do-it-yourself method suggested for matching holes to pegs is to clamp a stack of paper and/or cels to a drawing board. With an electric drill, drill three holes along one margin of the paper, allowing the drill to go into the drawing board too. Insert pegs into the drawing board holes. You'll have to agree this will assure proper alignment of holes and pegs. You

must also assure correct alignment of the holes you put in succeeding stacks of paper, or drill a new set of holes in the board each time around.

An easier method is to borrow or buy an ordinary three-hole paper punch like the ones used in offices and perforate your drawing sheets and cels with it. Then position a perforated sheet in the center of your drawing board and mark the perforations. Do the same on the animation stand baseboard. Drill holes at the marks and fasten register pegs in them.

In the two suggestions above, note that you can, if you wish, make one drawing board do double duty. Fasten register pegs into it and make your animation art. Then fasten the drawing board firmly to the animation stand so that it becomes the baseboard. Use the pegs for registering the artwork in the photographing stage.

Register pegs can be made from a variety of materials — round brass curtain rods, for example (Figure 42). If you are fortunate enough to know an electrician who discards old three-pronged plugs for electrical outlets, the round third plug used as a ground makes a dandy peg for registering animation cels.

Short lengths of 1/4-inch (6.3mm) wooden dowel, slightly tapered and rounded at the top, make very good pegs, as do wood screws. Select screws of a proper size to accommodate your cel perforations, screw them into the baseboard until only the smooth shaft protrudes; then cut off the screw heads with a hack saw and file smooth.

However you make them, it is important that the pegs fit the cel perforations snugly — loose enough to allow the sheets to go readily on and off but not so loose as to allow the sheets to move about laterally.

Professional register pegs and *peg bars* to hold them can be purchased, of course. These can be taped to the baseboard and drawing board or fitted into slots cut into them. Peg bars have the advantage of being movable to accommodate different fields of vision. They are available with scaled markings to aid in calibrating movements.

Peg bars are also expensive for the beginner. The pegs consist of one round peg flanked by two oblong pegs with flat sides. There are two types of peg sets — *Acme* and *Oxberry* — with the design of the pegs similar but nevertheless different. Bars with Acme pegs are generally used in the western part of the United States; Oxberry pegs are standard on the East Coast. This means you are not only faced with the cost of buying one or more sets of peg bars; you must buy drawing paper and cels with perforations to fit them, making sure you order the proper type each time.

While thinking of holding your artwork in place on the stand, also consider the clear platen that holds it flat. A loose glass plate will do, of course, but a faster and safer setup is one in which the glass or plastic is held in a hinged frame, so that it can be raised and lowered with ease and without danger of lateral movements. Suggestions for such a frame are shown in Figures 40 and 41.

CHOOSING A CAMERA

Before starting to plan or build an animation stand, think first about the camera you will use in it. This may determine some of the features of your stand, especially its dimensions.

In animation you will be photographing your subjects on a long reel of movie film and using a motion picture camera. However, you must

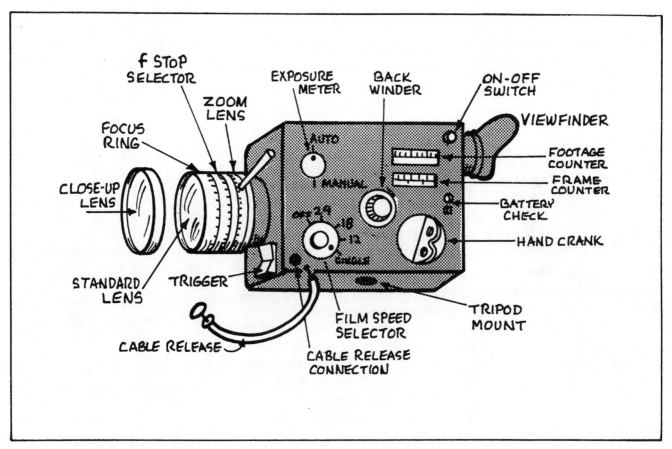

FOCUS RING

f STOP SELECTOR

ZOOM LENS

EXPOSURE METER

BACK WINDER

ON-OFF SWITCH

VIEWFINDER

CLOSE-UP LENS

AUTO

MANUAL

FOOTAGE COUNTER

FRAME COUNTER

BATTERY CHECK

HAND CRANK

STANDARD LENS

TRIGGER

FILM SPEED SELECTOR

TRIPOD MOUNT

CABLE RELEASE

CABLE RELEASE CONNECTION

Fig. 43 *Your camera doesn't have to have all these features, but each one adds to the potential and ease of what you can do.*

operate it like a conventional still camera, shooting one picture at a time. Between exposures some small change is made in the drawings or objects being photographed to obtain a progressive portrayal of motion. The process continues until all the frames required to complete a particular action are exposed.

Thus we see the necessity of working with a movie camera equipped for single-frame action (Figure 43). The camera will have a small hole at its side or front into which a cable release is fastened. The cable release is a plastic- or cloth-covered spring enclosing a flexible wire. A push button is at one end. Each time the button is pressed, the wire trips the shutter. The camera exposes one frame and moves the film forward to the next frame. Cable releases can be purchased for as little as a dollar. But

before you get a cheap one, consider how often you will be pressing that little button — literally hundreds of times for even a short film. You'll be better off spending a little more for a durable cable release.

Another important feature to consider when obtaining a camera is the viewfinder. Cameras in general have one or the other of two types of viewfinders, reflex and non-reflex. A reflex viewfinder is the most desirable, because it permits you to look directly through the lens. You can get in close to the artwork or objects on the animation stand and, more important, what you see in the viewfinder is exactly what will appear in the exposed frame, no more and no less.

The non-reflex viewfinder is separate from the lens. When you are

lining up your subject for photographing, this type of viewfinder may not show you the exact position or outer limits of what the lens will record — especially if you are shooting at very close range. The reason for this is that since the viewfinder is mounted separate from the lens, its optical axis is to the side or above the optical axis of the lens. This can result in positioning errors when framing subject matter, a state of affairs called *parallax*, a dirty word in animation and movie making.

Parallax can be a time-consuming problem for the animator working with three-dimensional subjects. The framing of puppets or objects must continually be checked and compensated for. At close range, a non-reflex viewfinder poses the threat of a partially decapitated puppet or an object that has been accidentally cropped out of the picture. If you *do* work with a camera with a non-reflex lens system and *are* working with three-dimensional objects, it is best to practice "setting your sights" and aiming before you get down to the serious business of shooting your planned film. Expose several test frames and study the results before proceeding with the many exposures required to make your film.

The problem of parallax is less critical when you are working with flat artwork. After an initial checking and positioning of the art in relation to the camera lens, your framing is reasonably secure until the next change of scene and/or focus.

And now for the good news. Nearly all movie cameras manufactured today, from 8mm up, are equipped with reflex lenses and viewfinders. It is only when you are working with older cameras — borrowed or purchased secondhand — that you may have to contend with a non-reflex system.

CAMERA SIZES

Motion picture cameras vary considerably in size, quality, and the features built into them. In this book, for reasons of economical animation, we will be discussing only 8mm, Super 8, and 16mm models. (Some mention is made of 35mm film in Chapter 5, but not many beginners have this expensive, professional-size camera readily at hand.)

Super 8 and 8mm

The principal difference between the Super 8 and 8mm cameras is in how they are loaded. The Super 8 accepts a cartridge; most 8mm cameras must be loaded with a reel of film. There is also a difference in the size of the individual frames (image areas) on the film. The Super 8 frame is larger even though both films are 8mm wide.

Beyond these basic differences, the Super 8 and 8mm cameras have a number of identical features and identical options. Depending on your purpose and how much money you want to invest, both cameras can come equipped with single-frame action and reflex viewfinders. Both can have the ability for manual or automatic lens changes.

Movie camera aficionados will tell you the Super 8 is capable of better definition than the 8mm. On the other hand, the reel-loaded 8mm has a *windback* facility not always available in cartridge-loaded cameras. This feature enables you literally to wind back the film in the camera and reshoot previously exposed frames to obtain interesting deliberate double exposures. Even when the windback is available in a Super 8 cartridge, it may be limited to about 100 frames. But this is enough to do a *fade* or a quick *dissolve* into another picture.

Despite this question of windback, if you are going to buy a new camera, you would be wise to opt for Super 8. Some manufacturers have stopped making the 8mm models and are

Fig. 44 A zoom lens makes it easy for you to move in from a medium shot (left) to a close-up.

concentrating improvements and new technology on the Super 8. If, however, you are pinching pennies, there are still plenty of excellent secondhand 8mm cameras available. And 8mm film to fit them should be around for some time to come.

The 16mm

A more professional camera, and more costly, is the 16mm model. This camera has a larger film size and a greater selection of types of film. What's more, present processing equipment and techniques permit some special optical effects with the 16mm that are not easily obtained with smaller sized films. Mechanically and optically, the 16mm will do everything a Super 8 and 8mm will do and more, including providing for interchangeable motors.

However, the use of a 16mm camera may be determined by your budget. There is a giant step from 8mm to double that size. The original cost of a 16mm camera, plus a corresponding increase in the cost of processing the larger film, may be more than you wish to consider at this time. Better to start small and grow with the business. Most beginning animators start with Super 8 or 8mm and graduate to 16mm as their accumulated knowledge and skill take them out of the beginner class.

Incidentally, you can be reasonably sure that any camera you obtain will have a standard ¼-inch (6.3mm) threaded hole for use in attaching it to tripods. With a matching bolt incorporated into the holder on your stand, you can use any camera that comes to hand. It's best to check first, though.

LENSES

Most cameras can be equipped, interchangeably, with several kinds of lenses — standard, zoom, telephoto, wide angle, fish-eye, and more. Standard and zoom lenses are the only ones that need concern the beginning animator.

A standard lens can accomplish just about everything you want to do, provided your animation stand is versatile enough to simulate certain movements. But what your stand can't do, a zoom lens can often do for you.

The most obvious example of this occurs when you wish to move (*zoom*) in close to a subject or back off from it (Figure 44). For you to move in close with a standard lens, your animation stand must be able to lower the entire camera a fraction of an inch between exposures. Conversely, to create the illusion of pulling away from the subject, the camera must be raised in the stand. A zoom lens, operated either manually or electrically, will accomplish both exercises as your camera remains locked in a fixed position. Zooming by camera or by lens alone is frequently used when figures in an animated film are shown walking toward or away from the viewer.

Obviously, then, if you don't have a zoom lens for your camera, be sure to build a "traveling" camera holder for your animation stand so that the camera can be raised or lowered.

FILM

Surprise! It's no more expensive to work with full color Super 8 and 8mm film than to shoot in black and white. Granted, a cartridge or reel of color film may cost a few cents more than one of black and white at this time, but most processing laboratories charge the same for developing either film. So you won't have to work your way up from black and white to full color as Walt Disney did. You can take the plunge into full color starting with Frame 1.

Film speed is an important factor to take into account when purchasing film in any size. The speed of a film is indicated by an ASA number and refers to the film's sensitivity to light. The higher the number, the more sensitive the film is. For example, a cartridge of Super 8 Ektachrome with an ASA of 160 will need less light than Kodachrome II marked ASA 40.

You will probably learn through experience that, when you are working at close quarters with a high intensity light source (such as two photoflood lamps on your animation stand), a film with an ASA of 40 will be sufficient for a good quality production. In fact, it may prove to be the most effective for you, but your animation stand and lighting arrangement will ultimately determine this.

SHOOTING AND FOCUSING

Here are some additional factors affecting your selection of a camera and its operation:

SHUTTER SPEED — Automatic or manual speed controls on cameras aren't factors in animation since shooting is done one frame at a time. You must, however, know the *shutter speed* so that you can read a *light meter* and adjust the *lens aperture* to the right setting. Movie cameras taking live action films generally operate at approximately 1/50 second, but slow down to a comparative snail's pace (¼ second) for single-frame action. A test film to check shutter speed and lens settings will prevent future headaches.

LENS OPENING — Somebody got things all turned around when they devised the system for marking lens apertures on cameras. The smaller the number is, the bigger the opening. Called *f stops*, they usually range from f/1.4 to f/32. You have to remember that the higher the setting, the less light the lens will allow in to expose your film. If you don't have a camera with an automatic exposure system, get a light meter and learn to use it. When adjusting the setting on your camera, first open the lens wide, to f/1.4, then stop down to the f stop the light meter tells you is needed. Also remember to set the ASA (film speed number) on the camera, unless that is an automatic feature.

DEPTH OF FIELD — This three-dimensional factor need not concern the animator working with flat artwork. But it can be a big problem when you are working with puppets and other three-dimensional objects. Depth of field is the distance between the closest object seen in focus in the viewfinder and the farthest one also in focus. If the camera is focused on the middle distance, for example, objects in the foreground may appear fuzzy and out-of-focus.

This is very pronounced when you are filming in the close measurements used in animation.

Don't despair. Careful plotting of object and puppet movements within the camera's field of vision will avoid much of the problem. Also consider that the problem can be turned to your advantage in some instances. Attention can be drawn to the star of the action by keeping it in sharp clarity in contrast to out-of-focus objects around it.

8

ANIMATING WITH A VIDEO CAMERA

Just about everything dealt with in this book concerning cartoon and object animation with a movie camera can also be accomplished with a *camcorder* (the buzzword for *video camera*), with the exception of recording sound that will synchronize with your visuals. Sound can be achieved, however, with special equipment and a measure of ingenuity.

As a matter of fact, many animation professionals claim that single-frame video is an ideal medium for learning and producing animation. But take care! These are pros talking. They are men and women who are in the "business" of producing animation. They work in production studios or educational and industrial production centers and are accustomed to using expensive equipment and techniques. You may find the cost of doing animation with a camcorder — including the camera, tape, animation stand, and other standard needs — to be prohibitive. The cost of developing film is eliminated, but video animation is still more expensive than animation with a movie camera.

USING A CAMCORDER

While most of the equipment and procedures described in the preceding and following chapters apply equally to a camcorder, no specific instructions can be given here for operating the camera itself. This is because of several differences among the makes and models of camcorders. Some are not capable of single-frame recording. Among those that are, some will do more than others and, as might be expected, the ones that do more, cost more. All have different arrangements and locations of controls and buttons to press. Hence, if you beg, borrow, or purchase a camcorder for the purpose of doing animation, the best advice you can follow is to read the operating manuals of several before deciding which to choose.

Assuming you have found a camcorder that suits your purpose, also make sure that it has some rigid, repeat rigid, means of support. You must fasten it firmly to a tripod or an animation stand. Most camcorders have a bolt or bolt hole at the bottom of the camera similar to the ones on movie cameras. It is extremely important that the camera does not move the slightest bit during the course of taping a single-frame animation sequence.

The danger of camera movement is lessened on the better camcorders by a remote control feature (Figure 44-a). But even with this feature, some cameras have an extra button or two that must be pressed to do the job.

The tripods available for supporting camcorders are usually sturdier than those used for movie cameras. If you choose to use a tripod for your camera support, it can be anchored to the floor by any of the methods shown in Figure 50.

You will also have to adjust, according to the camcorder you use, your calculations for timing and the number of frames to be shot of a single drawing or position of an object. Generally, camcorder manuals suggest shooting two to five shots of each setup. The time lapse must be taken into account, too. For example, the instructions for shooting objects with one popular make of camcorder say: "Move the object slightly and press the thumb trigger once for each 1-second recording in this position." When you consider that animation

on movie film requires 18 or 24 frames for each second of projection time, you can see that some adjustments of calculations must be made to avoid slow or jerky video animation.

One advantage shooting with a camcorder has over the movie camera is its "instant replay" feature. You can view your tape on a VCR without waiting for film to be developed. This means, however, that you must avoid mistakes from start to finish. When shooting with a movie camera, you can snip bungled frames out of the film and splice in corrected retakes.

Another feature of some camcorder models goes the "instant replay" one better. They come with (or

you can purchase) a cable attachment that can be plugged into a TV set, allowing you to view your taping step-by-step as you proceed. This practice of viewing the work in progress has been used in professional animation studies for several years, particularly in computer-assisted animation.

The sum of all this is to suggest that video animation is not for everyone, yet it may be just your cup of tea. If you want to venture into it, first consult with a person at a camcorder dealership who is a knowledgeable camcorder user, not just a salesperson. If you're lucky, your local high school or college art department may have courses in video that include animation.

Fig. 44-A *Some camcorders have a cable attachment allowing you to view your single-frame taping while work is in progress.*

9

ANIMATING THREE-DIMENSIONAL OBJECTS

It was mentioned at the beginning of this book that animation tricks the eye and thus can do the "impossible" things that live-action motion pictures can't do. This is particularly evident when one sees ordinary objects cutting capers on the screen. Cereal boxes pop open, mops wring themselves out, hamburgers talk, and tops unscrew from ketchup bottles. Television commercials are loaded with this sort of three-dimensional capering. Dolls and puppets are often used as well as objects.

For the beginning animator, three-dimensional or *object animation* may prove the easiest initiation into the process of single-frame shooting with a movie camera. Of course, this is provided that you start with simple objects and that the planned action is not too complicated.

Object animation follows a routine similar to that used in cel animation, but it eliminates the necessity of tedious and time-consuming preparation of artwork. Instead of a series of drawings on cels, the object itself is moved and photographed one frame at a time. As in all other filmed animation, 18 or 24 frames must be exposed to obtain one second of film. That great little helper, persistence of vision, also applies, so you don't have to move the object in every frame. You can shoot on *twos* or on *threes*, meaning you change the position of an object every two or three frames.

Successful object animation *does* require careful advance planning, preferably sketched out on a *storyboard*, a series of quick sketches indicating the key points of the action. Advance thought should also be given to lighting, the size and scope of the *background*, and the location of props and extra scenery. In effect, you will be creating and working in a Lilliputian movie set.

OBJECTS FOR ANIMATION

Nobody wants to put a damper on your talent, but perhaps at the start you would be better off animating simple objects instead of more intricate dolls and puppets. Even with ordinary items like buttons, paper clips, chess pieces, clothespins, or pencil sharpeners, the idea's the thing, and a little imagination can produce jumbo results (Figure 45). Or fashion your own objects with modeling clay (Plasticine) or ordinary potter's clay painted with poster colors.

You can manipulate objects just for the sake of seeing them in seemingly impossible antics. For example, you can make a sardine can open itself and a sardine slither out. Or you can animate objects in such a way as to tell a story. Figure 46 shows frames of the story-board for a short animated film about two dogs meeting on the street. Two leashes represent the dogs—a light leash for the female and a heavier collar and chain for the male. The leashes were moved about on a small area of clean floor and were filmed from above by a camera clamped to a stationary pipe. A zoom lens was used to obtain the close-ups.

REPRESENTATIONAL OBJECTS

The film of the two dog leashes illustrates a frequently used technique in object animation — using various items to represent people or animals. In this case, nothing had to be done to the leashes in order for them to depict imaginary dogs. In the same vein, two pairs of shoes or two hats could be filmed to show an encounter between two persons. The size and styles of the shoes or hats would indicate the types of persons who "filled" them.

Faces and clothing can also be painted on inanimate objects to create "characters" for your films (Figure 47). Or the objects can be personalized with stick-on faces (made of paper or felt) and provided with arms and legs made of materials such as soda straws, pipe cleaners, toothpicks, and modeling clay.

PUPPETS AND DOLLS

Animation successes with objects will undoubtedly lead you to try your hand at producing three-dimensional animation on a more grand scale. That means obtaining or making puppets and dolls to people your films.

You can also purchase at toy stores various character dolls, complete with extensive wardrobes, if you wish to launch a "big budget production."

There are drawbacks to using ready-made dolls and puppets, how-

Fig. 45 With the addition of paper ears and tusks, pencil sharpeners make dandy elephants.

ever. The first is that, even though their heads will move, you can't change their expressions. Changing expressions is especially important if your film calls for dialogue.

A larger drawback is that ready-made dolls don't give you an opportunity to create really imaginative characters that can be manipulated at will and their expressions changed to suit the action. Besides, it's more fun to make your own.

You can make puppets out of a variety of materials — wood, corks, Styrofoam, Popsicle sticks, wire, pipe cleaners, nuts, fruits, vegetables, papier-mâché, and modeling clay, to name a few. In some instances you can use potter's clay, but it tends to be crumbly and will quickly dry out and stiffen under the heat of your floodlamps when being filmed. The stiffening can be retarded to some

extent by mixing petroleum jelly with the clay before making your puppet.

Here are some other things to consider when making puppets for animation:

Size

An animated puppet should be small enough to manipulate easily, but large enough so that facial expressions can be seen. Remembering that a recommended distance from the camera to the center of the action is 3 feet or more (about 1 meter), consider your puppets in relation to what action must take place within the camera's field of vision. If they are too small, the action will be lost in a large background like an ant on a dinner plate. If they are too large, you won't be able to move them about without decapitating them or otherwise losing some of

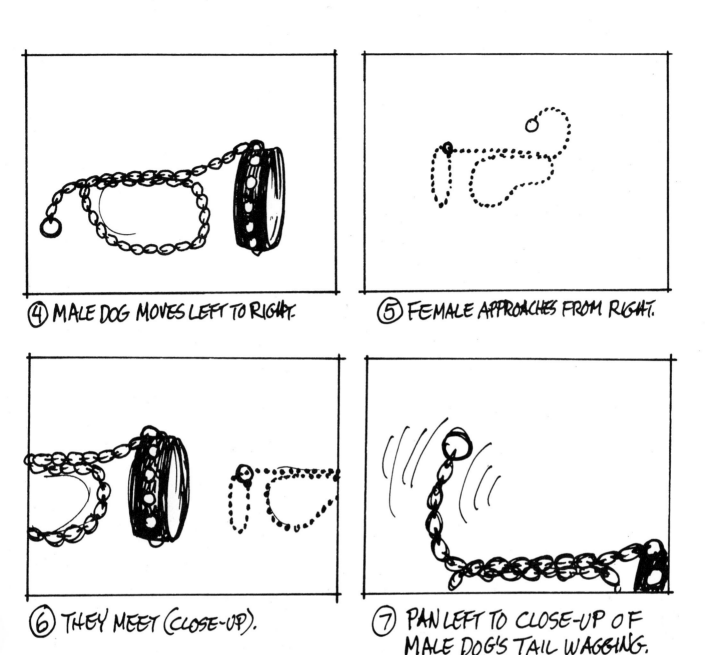

④ MALE DOG MOVES LEFT TO RIGHT.

⑤ FEMALE APPROACHES FROM RIGHT.

⑥ THEY MEET (CLOSE-UP).

⑦ PAN LEFT TO CLOSE-UP OF MALE DOG'S TAIL WAGGING.

Fig. 46 *Four sketches from a rough storyboard for a film about two dogs. Only dog leashes and a collar were used against a blank background.*

their actions. This is why pre-planning is always advisable in three-dimensional animation.

If a puppet figure is too tall, you may also have trouble keeping it from toppling, which leads us to consider …

Stability

Always be certain to make a puppet with a firm enough base to keep it upright and unmoving while you are filming (Figure 48). (This is a principal reason that many ready-made dolls cannot be used for animation.) Every move an object or a part of an object makes, even the slightest vibration, will be recorded by the camera in subsequent frames. This means your puppet must stand firm while you are making changes in the facial expression, tilting the head, making adjustments in arm movements, or creating other actions called for in your film.

Strength

If modeling in clay, don't sacrifice the strength of a puppet's moving parts in order to ensure the stability of the rest of the figure. If you make an arm too bendable, it may sag or even break off during shooting. It's a good idea to construct your clay figures over *armatures*, little stick figures made of wire. Be certain, of course, that the moving portions of the figures are modeled on sufficiently limber wire so that you can move them easily and repeatedly.

Exaggeration

For the sake of stability, you may find yourself building puppets with extraordinarily large feet. Don't fret about it. This can prove to be a blessing in disguise. Unless you are very skilled at sculpture or wood-carving, it will be difficult for you to fashion puppets that are lifelike. Even if you can, you will find that puppets that closely resemble the human face tend to look cold and lifeless on the screen.

So don't try to copy life accurately. Instead, people your films with simple, stylized characters with exaggerated features and body parts. Give them uniquely shaped torsos and feet big enough to trample out grass fires. Deepen the scowl of the villain, thicken the neck of the tough guy, square the jaw of the hero. They'll look and act more as you intend them to. You need only study the multitude of exaggerated characters on "Sesame Street" to see how this comes true.

BUILDING SETS

A prime consideration in designing a set for puppet animation is to provide a little bit more. It may be starkly simple or extremely ornate — depending on the story and mood you wish to convey. In any case, your set, like the puppets in it, should be scaled to the field of vision of your camera setup and the action that takes place within that frame. Your set should always extend a bit beyond the frame for safety's sake.

Even if you plan to film puppets in no setting at all, you should provide a plain background of white, gray, or color that is at least a bit larger than the camera's field. Try,

for example, backing your characters with a brick wall, a sheet of not-too-ornate wallpaper, or a velvet drape.

Still working on the assumption that a little more than 3 feet (about 1 meter) is a handy distance from the camera to the objects being filmed, you'll find things work out better if you establish your camera's field *before* you build your set. First attach your camera to a stable tripod or an animation stand, then focus on the tabletop, shelf, or other baseboard where your puppets will act out their roles. A look through the camera's viewfinder will show you the area that will be exposed on film. Mark this area and take its measurements for use when making the set.

The width, height, and forward area of the set should be large enough to extend outside the camera's view (Figure 49). This is to avoid unsightly and unexplained blank spaces at the edges of the picture. It also provides areas of support for puppets that walk or otherwise move offstage. If you intend to pan the camera, that is to move its line of vision right or left or up and down to follow the action of a moving puppet, you must provide an additional area or areas on the set to accommodate the roving eye of the camera.

This is also true when you consider the visual possibilities of shooting from more than one angle. With the camera moved to different positions to add greater variety to your

Fig. 47 *A collection of objects, including two "personalized" champagne corks, showing how various things around the home can be used in animation. The coffee cups starred in a film entitled* A Coupla Mugs.

film, you must be sure there is adequate set area to fill the various fields of vision.

Always establish your initial field of vision as if shooting a long shot, because it requires the most background area. Then you won't have to worry about having enough set when you zoom in for medium shots and close-ups.

Materials

Your choice of design and selection of materials for sets offer as much opportunity for variety and imagination as the making of puppets. Styrofoam, cardboard, gift boxes, sponges, clay, corks, tin cans, and fabric remnants combined with poster paints and felt markers can produce almost any desired locale. A sandbox makes a credible Sahara Desert, and a rectangle of green carpet is a dandy puppet-sized front lawn. Don't overlook the scenic possibilities in a borrowed doll house and doll furniture.

CAMERA SETUPS

More often than not, amateur three-dimensional animation of puppets or objects is filmed with the camera on a tripod. This permits considerable flexibility in camera angles and more freedom than an animation stand would permit in the construction of backgrounds and sets. However, other types of camera arrangements can be used with good results.

Tripod

Camera tripods are not just for tired photographers. Their main function is to hold a camera steady, and this is never more important than when shooting the numerous frames needed for an animated film. Thus, it is essential that you use a sturdy tripod with all of its adjustment screws firmly tightened, and its legs

securely anchored on a non-skid surface.

There are several ways a tripod can be anchored. A triangular piece of non-slip carpet or 1 inch (2.54cm) thick foam rubber often will serve the purpose. The piece can be rolled up and stored when not in use.

To make doubly sure, however, make a tripod holder of wood. It will remain firm and won't stretch out of shape. Two suggested designs are shown in Figure 50, though there are many other variations. To establish the dimensions of the basic triangle, first adjust your tripod and camera to the height from which you will be shooting, then take measurements for the holder.

Note that holes are drilled at the corners so the tripod feet can be set into them. To avoid tripod scratches on the floor, do not drill the holes all the way through the wood. If you will be working on a waxed or highly polished floor, glue some skid-resistant pads on the bottom of the tripod holder.

Look around your work area and you may find other opportunities for anchoring your camera. A stepladder, providing it's a steady one, can serve as a make-do tripod. Drill a hole through one step and insert a bolt to secure the camera. Basement workrooms often have exposed pipes to which a camera can be clamped.

Lights

In all types of camera setups, with a tripod or otherwise, remember that you must also provide for two floodlamps to light your set. You can buy inexpensive clamps in camera shops and hardware stores that will attach the lamps to a variety of supports.

Both lights should be mounted so that they point downward at the set at

Fig. 48 *This clay figure was given big feet for extra stability.*

Fig. 49 *(following page) Two three-dimensional sets using a camera on a tripod. Note that the background in each case extends well beyond the field of vision.*

an angle, usually 45 degrees, to minimize shadows and reflections. The lights should be secured in the same place during the filming of an entire scene, and in most cases the entire film, to ensure uniform exposure and contrasts.

A dimming device on your light switch will permit you to fade in and fade out a scene as the Hollywood types do.

SOME DO'S AND DON'TS

• Plan and shoot your first three-dimensional animated film with the camera in a fixed position. Later, with more experience and confidence, you can successfully

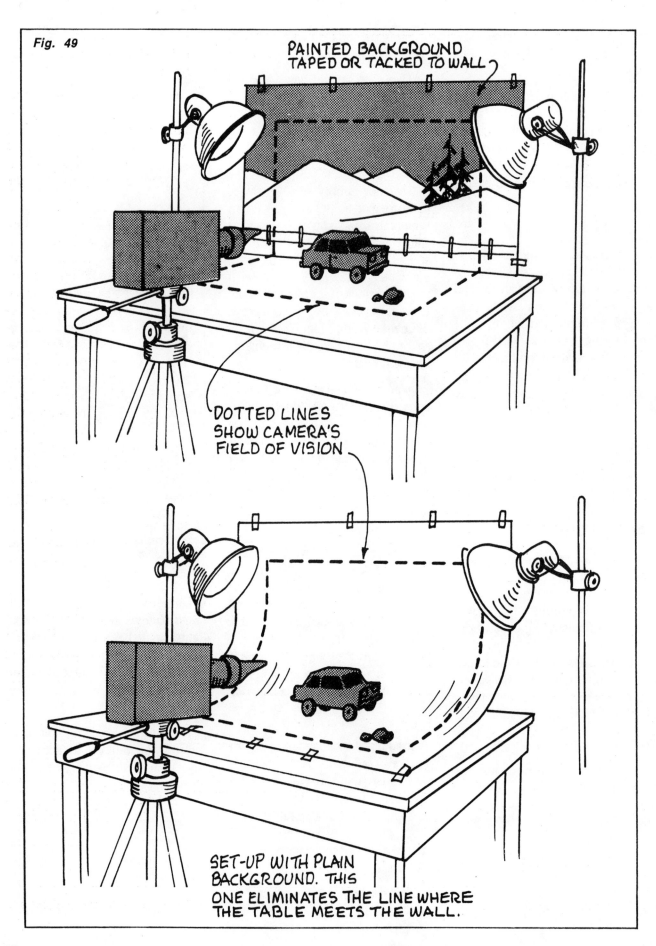

Fig. 49

PAINTED BACKGROUND
TAPED OR TACKED TO WALL

DOTTED LINES
SHOW CAMERA'S
FIELD OF VISION

SET-UP WITH PLAIN
BACKGROUND. THIS
ONE ELIMINATES THE LINE WHERE
THE TABLE MEETS THE WALL.

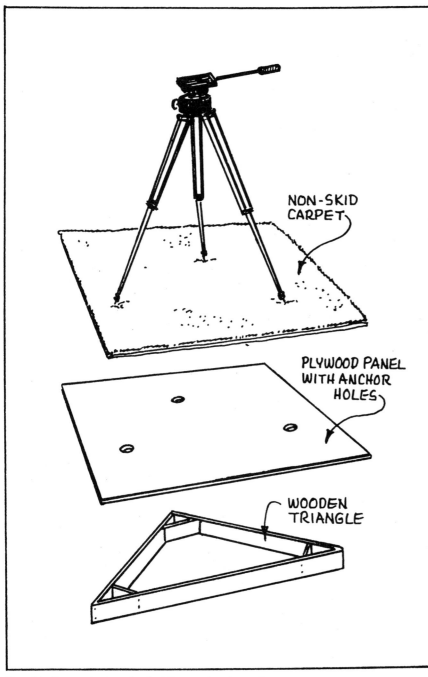

NON-SKID
CARPET

PLYWOOD PANEL
WITH ANCHOR
HOLES

WOODEN
TRIANGLE

Fig. 50 *Some devices for holding a tripod steady.*

incorporate zooming, panning, and moving the camera to different angles.

- Three-dimensional animation should almost always be shot on threes or less. If you shoot four or more frames between movements of objects, your film will appear jerky (like an old Charlie Chaplin movie).

- Another jerky problem to beware of is having the action start and stop too abruptly. Consider that if you walk across a room and stop on the other side, you will accelerate progressively from a standing start and will slow down before you come to a full stop. Similarly, your animated objects should start and stop at a slower pace than when at mid-point in a movement. This is called *slowing in* and *slowing out*, and it is best to chart it on paper (Figure 51) before you start filming. Slowing in and out makes animated action seem more natural and your film more professional.

- Slowing in and slowing out should also be used when panning the camera.

- Before charting any action on paper, actually put the object through the anticipated motion and time it with a stopwatch or the second hand of an ordinary watch. Re-

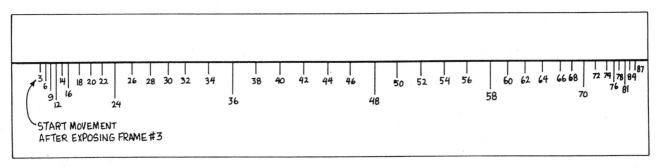

Fig. 51 *A slow in, slow out chart. It shows the numbers of the frames to be exposed and the distance the filmed object is to be moved each time.*

membering that you must shoot 24 frames for each second of projection time, you can quickly calculate how many frames are needed to accomplish each action. With this number in hand, you can determine how many times the object must be moved from start to finish.

- Camera focus (depth of field) is very critical when filming at close quarters. Keep this in mind when pre-planning your three-dimensional actions. Keep front-to-back and back-to-front movements at a minimum, except when out-of-focus effects are desired.

- Patience, patience. At some stage of the filming, as you slowly inch an object across the set centimeter by centimeter, an almost uncontrollable yeast of impatience will begin to rise within you. You'll want to speed up the action and skip some of the movements. And the result will be just what you make it — a hurried, less than satisfactory film. It's better to go slower than necessary than too fast. So, curb your frustration. Hang up a GO SLOW sign where you work.

10

ANIMATING CUTOUTS

The technique of using cutout paper figures in animation is a direct descendant of the *silhouette* and *shadow films* popular in Europe around the turn of the century. In modern cutout animation, the lighting has been brought forward from behind the screen to illuminate the figures in front.

You can make a shadow film if you like, but you'll probably find it's more fun to work with front-lighted figures. A small quantity of paper, a pair of scissors, and some felt markers will put you in business. Of course, you'll also need a camera, lights, and a simple animation stand.

You don't have to limit your imagination to drawings on plain or colored paper. You can also combine them with bits of cloth, wallpaper, sandpaper, and other textured materials. A delightful animated film can be made of figures and objects cut from magazines or greeting cards. You can also combine these and/or drawings with photographs of yourself and friends.

GETTING STARTED

It would be easy to say, "Plan your story, cut out your figures, and start shooting." But when you are dealing with cutouts, as with other animation artwork, the camera's field of vision, the area you'll have to move the cutouts in, is most important. Therefore, it's not a bad idea to prepare an animation stand first, mount your camera, and establish its field

or fields of vision before launching the other enterprises.

CAMERA SETUP

Cutout animation is accomplished most easily in a vertical setup with the camera aimed straight down at artwork on a level baseboard. Some suggestions for simple animation stands you can make are shown in Figure 40 on page 52. They are also designed for filming cel animation, but for cutouts you won't have to bother with register pegs and peg bars. You should, however, provide for a glass platen to hold down the paper cutouts and eliminate disturbing shadows around the edges. To avoid hazardous shifting, and to speed lifting the platen each time you change the position of a cutout, hinge the glass plate along the top edge with a wide strip of tape. Be sure the tape and the edges of the glass are outside the camera field.

To avoid light reflections, mount two photoflood lamps above and to each side of the animation stand baseboard so that they are aimed at the glass at a 45 degree angle.

With the camera firmly bolted or clamped in place perpendicular to the filming area, the next step is to establish its field of vision in sharp focus on the baseboard (Figure 52). A convenient size for this field of action is 14" x 10" (about 33 x 25 cm). This means your camera would be located somewhere between 3 and 4 feet (122 and 91 cm) above the baseboard, depending on its type and lens. (This should be considered when building your stand.)

FOCUSING

Now, draw a dark X on a piece of paper and put it in the center of the baseboard under the platen. Get the X into sharp focus in your viewfinder and note the outer edges of the camera's range of vision. Make faint corner marks on the baseboard about ½ inch (1.27cm) outside the field. These outside measurements will serve as guides in establishing the size of your cutouts and any background you may draw or paint for them. The marks will also help you position the background and cutouts when filming.

The preceding paragraph presumes that you are using a camera with a through-the-lens viewfinder. If you have a non-reflex viewfinder, which is separate from the lens, you won't see quite the same area that the lens sees. This is that old bugaboo called parallax, and you'll have to make a correction to ensure that you mark the field of vision exactly where it really should be on the baseboard. Put a tiny dot in the center of the viewfinder's field of vision, then drop a plumb line from the camera lens. It will touch the baseboard a little to the side of the dot you have made.

Tilt the camera to compensate for the difference.

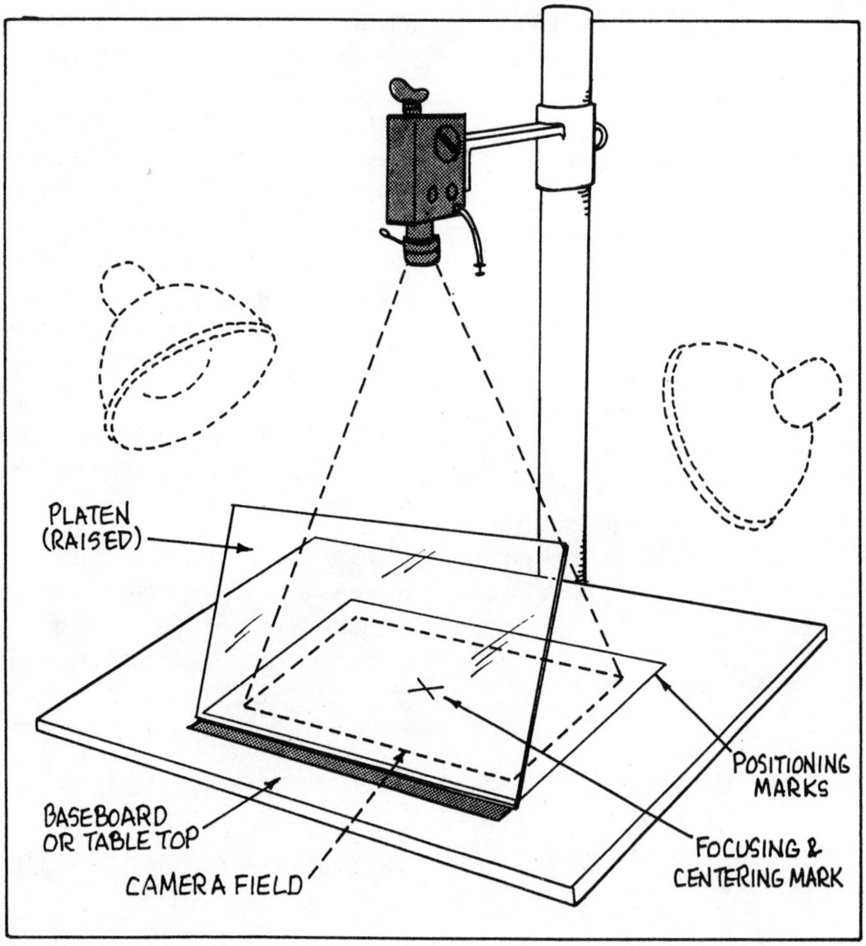

RAISING INTEREST LEVEL

From this point onward, the routine of animation with cutouts is quite similar to three-dimensional and cel animation (Chapters 9 and 11). It is a matter of photographing frame by frame a planned succession of movements made by paper cutouts rather than objects or a series of acetate cels. This can be humdrum undertaking; and the results can be humdrum, too, unless you inject some techniques that have proved effective in raising the interest level.

Study the animated cartoons on Saturday morning television — or even comic strips in your local newspaper — and you'll notice that the characters are frequently shown at different distances from the viewer. Sometimes they'll be standing full length. At other times you'll only see them from the waist up or will see an enlarged drawing of the head alone. These variations from long shots to close-ups add to the vibrancy and interest of comic strips, and they are particularly helpful for enhancing animated films.

If you have a zoom lens on your camera, you can easily vary your cutout animation simply by making adjustments for long, medium, and close-up shots. Another, more complex way is to construct an animation stand in which the camera can be moved up and down. Focal adjustments must be made at each level.

CUTOUTS IN THREE SIZES

A third way, which permits a fixed lens setting and a stationary camera, is to standardize the cutouts in three sizes, each scaled to the field of vision you have established. The three sizes are specifically designed for long, medium, and close-up shots.

Fig. 52 A simple animation stand set up for filming cutouts. An X has been marked at the center of the baseboard for establishing a sharp focus. The X and corner markings on the baseboard also help in positioning the cutouts.

Fig. 53 *Three cutouts of the same figure permit changing from a long shot to a medium shot and a close-up without a zoom lens and without moving the camera.*

An example of this is the walking man (Figure 53). If you filmed a few seconds of the action showing his full figure, then suddenly substituted the medium shot or the close-up of his head, the effect would be similar to making the changes with a zoom lens.

There are also some production advantages in working with different sized cutouts. For instance, when you are filming a medium shot or a close-up of a walking man, his legs aren't shown and you don't have to bother changing their positions every two or three frames. Another help (Figure 54) is that you can change the angle of the head at the same time that you switch from a long or medium shot to a close-up or vice versa, giving more variety to your animation.

These advantages were used to the fullest in a cutout film titled *The Physics Lesson*. Several frames of the film's storyboard are shown in Figure 55 to demonstrate the movement in and out from long shots to close-ups and the altering of head positions by substituting auxiliary cutouts.

DEPTH AND DISTANCE

Even though you are working in two dimensions with flat materials, you may wish to create the illusion of

motion that goes away from the camera or comes toward it. If done correctly, this can be even more exciting than the in-and-out cuts just described.

You needn't be told that objects close to you appear larger than the same objects seen in the distance, so the trick is to figure out how to shrink a character or object gradually as it moves away from the camera, or make it grow in size as it approaches. The trick, alas, is simply hard work. It requires that you do several cutouts of the same figure. Each must be scaled a little smaller or larger than the preceding one (Figure 56). If it is a moving person like the one shown in Figure 78 in Chapter 12, you must change the leg positions for each alternate cutout to simulate walking or running.

BACKGROUND ASSISTANCE

A little background planning will also help create the illusion of depth and distance. In the example shown in Figure 78, the background is a corridor down which the figure is walking. The vertical lines of the doors and the converging floor lines are arranged in proper perspective to create the desired illusion. This same feeling of distance is achieved in outdoor scenes with vertical lines of telephone poles, converging lines of

Fig. 54 *Design your medium shot cutouts so you can provide an extra head or two.*

Fig. 55 *Storyboard for a cutout film,* The Physics Lesson, *showing use of different size cutouts filmed on top of a moving (panning) background. The abbreviations CU, LS, and E-W are directions for close-up, long shot, and east-west.*

74

a road, and the spacing of ground lines (Figure 56) — all good exercises in the use of perspective.

Generally, the farther away and, therefore, the smaller an object is, the higher you should place it in the frame. This is especially true when you are using a blank background so that your cutouts will appear to come from or be moving toward a vanishing point on an imaginary horizon line.

CUTTING CORNERS WITH CUTOUTS

Just as limited animation saves a lot of drawing time in cel animation, you can reduce the amount of drawing and cutting you have to do in making cutouts by designing them with interchangeable parts. Imagine, for example, that you want to animate the cutout figure of a woman who speaks alternately to persons on either side of her, then speaks directly to the camera. There is no need to draw and cut out the figure of the woman three times. You need to do the figure only once and provide her with accessory heads (Figure 57). This particular lady is very talkative, so she has also been provided with a whole "wardrobe" of accessory mouths and facial features.

MORE DESIGN TIPS

- If your cutouts must move both right-to-left and left-to-right, it is easier and more accurate to draw identical details on the reverse side than to cut out a second figure facing in the opposite direction.

- When drawing cutouts, outline them in bold ink or felt marker lines (using finer lines, if you wish, for details). Thus, when cutting out the figures, you can cut along the middle of the heavy outline and avoid leaving unsightly extra paper around the edges.

- After cutting out a figure, paint the edges of the paper with the same ink or paint used for the outline. A white or light colored edge will accentuate any shadow that may occur when you are filming.

- Think carefully about the movements your cutouts will make and

Fig. 56 *Two ways to give the impression of distance through the use of different size cutouts. First, the skier moves in and out of view. Second, the bird sails to a close-up with the aid of progressively larger cutouts.*

Fig. 57 *Interchangeable parts save work and time. In the scene above, the head, eyes, and mouth of the talkative lady were the only cutouts that had to be manipulated.*

Fig. 58 *A line of demarcation between moving parts and the rest of a cutout saves work and time. In the figures above, the legs of the man and hippo can be moved without disturbing the bodies.*

design them so that the joinings of the moving parts are disguised. For example, the pearl necklace on the talkative lady (Figure 57) disguises the joining each time she is given a new head. In Figure 58 the hemline of the man's coat has been lowered to form a separation between body and moving legs. Similarly, a bold line separates the hippo's body and legs.

• When drawing and cutting out arms and legs that are inserted beneath the main cutout, provide extra length at the joining end to allow for movement.

• Cutouts can be as simple or as complex as you feel competent to handle. Figure 61 shows two ways to design legs for a walking figure. You may feel safer with the "wheel" arrangement, which is a simple adaptation of a child's toy. If you're in a bolder mood, try the four-stage arrangement.

A PLOT THAT QUICKENS

With cutouts, as with any other type of animation, time spent charting at the beginning will actually save time in the long run. Each type of animation has its own tactical problems as well.

In cutout animation a particular problem is the correct placing of loose paper figures for each successive movement. You may in your mind's eye envision a simple hop of a kangaroo across the screen. But when it comes to actually placing the kangaroo at each point of his arc, you can't jump to conclusions. First, you must plot the arc, a normal animation procedure. But in cutout animation you also should devise a method for keeping the paper cutout on the arc. The answer is a template, or templates. Following are two suggestions for making them.

TEMPLATE POSITIONING GUIDES

The kind of template easiest to use in cutout animation is made of cardboard or illustration board. It should be slightly thicker than the paper you use for cutouts, and a little larger at the sides and bottom than the camera field.

Plot the arc of the kangaroo hop on the cardboard and cut away the portion above the line (Figure 59). Mark along this curving edge the points where the bottom of the cutout kangaroo should be at each stage of the action. (Remember the advice about slowing in and slowing out.)

Hinge the template to the animation stand baseboard, using tape along its base. Each time you must change the position of the kangaroo, swing the template over into the camera field and line up the cutout at the next mark.

Another type of template can be made from a clear sheet of acetate slightly larger than the camera field. It, too, should be attached at the bottom with a tape hinge. Chart the movements of your cutout right on the acetate and, each time you change the position of a cutout, check the position by lowering the transparent template over it. Do the charting with a grease pencil or non-permanent felt marker so that the marks can be wiped off and the template can be used again and again.

ANIMATED WALKING — STEP-BY-STEP

Walking is perhaps the most frequently used action of animated persons and animals. In a majority of instances, the cutouts are shown walking on a horizontal line across the screen from left to right and right to left. You can produce this lateral movement in either of two methods:

1. Literally move the walking figure from one side of the camera field to the other, changing the leg positions as it goes.

2. Keep the figure and moving legs in a fixed spot under the lens and move the background behind them. This method permits longer walks, because it is limited only by the length of the panoramic background you provide.

In either case, the number of cutouts and the leg movements are identical. You need a cutout of the body and four cutouts of leg positions. The leg pieces are used in a four-stage cycle to make one full step, and you can repeat the cycle to lengthen the walk.

The difference between animating a walk against a stationary background and against a moving one is whether or not the whole body is moved. A different type of template is used to control each method. Let's start with the shortest walk.

WALK CYCLE WITH STATIONARY BACKGROUND

A first step (pardon the pun) is to establish a rate at which you want the cutout figure to move.

Let's assume the camera field is 14 inches (35.5cm) across, and 2 inches (5cm) is the widest spread of the leg cutouts for your walking man,

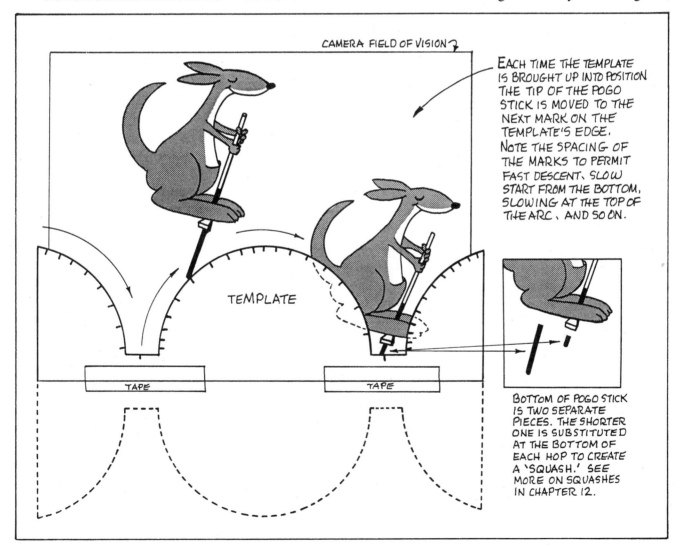

Fig. 59 A hinged paper template is used here to guide the leaps of a kangaroo. Note that he leaves the ground more gradually than he lands, slowing down at the top of the arc.

meaning that's the length of one full stride. In seven full strides you can move him from one side of the camera field to the other. Using four leg positions and shooting them on twos (double framing), you'll have him striding along at a brisk pace.

Having set the pace, next make a cardboard template that looks something like a ruler (Figure 60). The template should be 14 inches (35.5cm) long, or more. Every 2 inches (5.08cm) along the top edge should be marked and numbered. Place the template on the baseboard so that the marked edge is on an imaginary horizontal line along which the walking man will tread. Make the template with enough depth for its bottom to be well out of the camera field. Hinge it to the baseboard with tape.

Now we are ready to shoot the cutouts. Use the four leg combinations shown in Figure 61 as your guide. Figure 60 shows how the procedure goes:

1. With the template in guide position, place cutout No. 1 (legs at full stride) at the starting point.

In this case we've chosen mark No. 2 on the template. The heel of the leading foot should be right on the mark. Center the body cutout on the legs. Swing the template down out of the way. Lower your platen to hold the cutouts flat. Shoot two frames.

2. Swap platen and template, and substitute leg cutout No. 2. As before, the heel of the front foot should touch the No. 2 mark on the template. Note that this leg, which bears the body's weight, has swung forward at the top about ½ inch (1.25cm). The body cutout should be moved forward with it. Shoot two frames.

3. Repeat the exchange with leg cutout No. 3, moving the body along with the top portion of the legs. Shoot two frames.

4. Repeat with leg cutout No. 4. Note that the heel of the swinging leg has moved forward almost to the No. 3 mark on the template and is about to complete the full stride. Shoot two frames.

5. Substitute leg cutout No. 1 with the leading heel at mark No. 3. This completes the first cycle and, at the same time, is the first position of the next cycle. Because the leg cutouts are in solid color and no separation is shown between the legs, the near leg in the first cycle now becomes the leg on the far side. If you draw legs in outline and show the separation (as in Figure 62), you will have to make eight cutouts of legs instead of four.

WALK CYCLE WITH MOVING BACKGROUND

As was mentioned earlier, the other method of animating a walk is to keep the figure in a fixed spot and move the background laterally behind it. The body and leg cutouts can be identical in either method, but different kinds of templates are used to control the position of the walking figure.

For the purpose of explaining the moving backgrounds method, we will use the same timing for the movements that was used in the section immediately preceding this one

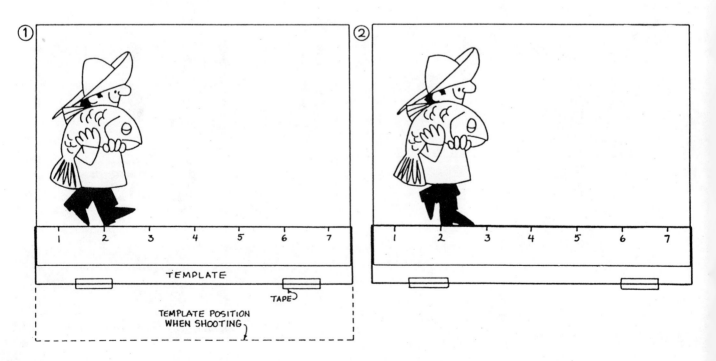

— that is, a full stride of 2 inches (5.08cm) and shooting on twos. Our walking figure, in this case, however, is a lady with an umbrella. And we'll use eight leg cutouts to show the movement of one leg behind the other.

As shown in Figure 62, the body cutout remains in a fixed position under the camera. The leg cutouts are changed after every pair of exposures and the panoramic background is moved ½ inch (1.25cm) at a time in the direction opposite to that in which the lady is walking.

Again, a hinged template is used. But this one is designed to keep the lady in her place. The template should be made of cardboard slightly thicker than the paper cutouts. Hinge it at the bottom with tape well outside the camera field.

The top of the template should be horizontal. A shallow notch is cut into it, and this indentation should be just wide enough to accommodate the hemline of the lady's coat. Fasten the template to the baseboard so that her body will be correctly positioned when it is placed in the notch (see dotted lines in Figure 62).

To maintain the desired pace of the walk cycle, a ruler-like scale is again used. This time it will guide the movement of the background instead of the legs. The scale should be marked like a ruler along the top edge of the background, which is drawn or painted on a long strip of paper. When this panorama is in position for the first exposure, put a mark on the baseboard immediately next to the scale. The fixed mark (usually directly above the walking figure) will be your guide when shifting the background.

With the background in place and the cutouts ready at hand, start the routine of filming thus:

1. With the aid of the hinged template, position the body cutout on the background. Swing the template out of the way and carefully slide the first leg cutout into position. Part of it will be under the body. Lower the platen. Shoot two frames.

2. Replace the template, then move the background ½ inch (1.25cm) to the left. The template will hold the body in place.

3. Remove the template. Insert the second leg cutout. Lower the platen and shoot two more frames.

Continue in this manner through the entire cycle of eight leg cutouts. Repeat the cycles as often as you wish. The illusion will be that the little lady is walking along and the camera is keeping pace with her along the street.

SKIP IT

If you add one more detail, you can give the lady's walk an extra fillip that really makes it come alive. It's a little hopping skip in her stride.

It's easy. During every other cycle, when shooting leg cutouts 2 and 3, simply move the body and leg cutouts ½ inch (1.25cm) higher in the frame. Bring them back down to the original level within the template notch when substituting leg cutout No. 4.

HANDLING CUTOUTS

Use a pair of tweezers when changing the paper cutouts. This makes the

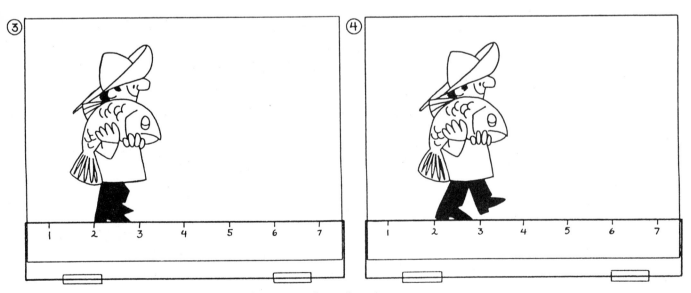

Fig. 60 Use of a hinged template to control the pace of a walk cycle.

79

positioning easier and more accurate. It prevents the accidental bumping of other cutouts in the frame. And it keeps fingerprints and smudges from your artwork.

When using a glass platen or templates, raise it slowly and carefully to avoid "sucking up" cutouts and moving them out of place. If you have trouble with this, put a blob of rubber cement on your finger, wait until it is tacky, and roll it into a tiny ball. Put this bit of cement under the vagrant cutout and press down. The "stickum" can be removed later without damage to the cutout or background.

LIGHTING FOR CUTOUTS

Photoflood lamps can generate a lot of heat when left on for some time. If

Fig. 61 *Two ways to design cutout legs to animate a walk.*

they are too close to the baseboard, or if you work too long without turning them off, the heat may cause your cutouts to curl. This is another reason the glass platen is recommended.

One way to prevent heat-curl from floodlamps is to experiment with the use of two 150-watt incandescent bulbs instead. You'll need a wider aperture setting, of course, but the controlled conditions of an animation stand permit such experiments. Shoot a few frames of film under selected lighting conditions and judge the results before going ahead with a proposed film.

This is as good a time as any to remind you to make sure the camera's lens is clean and free of fingerprints before starting each shooting sequence.

MOVING (PANNING) BACKGROUND IS DRAWN ON LONG HORIZONTAL STRIP OF PAPER. SCALE AT TOP (OUT OF FIELD OF VISION) AND ARROW MARK ON BASEBOARD ARE USED TO REGULATE THE SPEED OF BACKGROUND MOVEMENTS.

BACKGROUND MOVES TO LEFT.

TAPE

TEMPLATE

HEMLINE ON RAINCOAT

① ② ③ ④ ⑤ ⑥ ⑦ ⑧

Fig. 62 Use of a hinged template to position a cutout during a walk cycle with a moving background. If legs are drawn in outline, instead of opaque silhouettes, eight sets must be drawn and cut out in order to show one leg moving behind the other.

SOUND ADVICE

Your first cutout animation may be a silent film, or perhaps have a musical background added on. Or you may plunge right into dialogue, using recorded voices (see Chapter 15).

Making a silent film doesn't stop you from using dialogue, however. Do what comic-strip artists do. Put the words in speech balloons and pop the balloons on and off the screen as each of your characters says his or her piece. Examples of this are shown in Figures 55 (page 74) and 63. Of course, the balloon must be held on the screen long enough for it to be read and understood, so keep the sentences short.

You can emphasize a statement by zooming in on a balloon or cutting to a close-up of it. When characters shout, the lettering in the balloons should be BIG and **BOLD**. When they whisper, make it small. Various letter styles — delicate, bold, ornate, rough — also can be used to enhance the personalities of the speakers.

If you opt for full sound and dialogue, your film will almost certainly require that you learn to do *lip-sync*. This is the process of *synchronization* of the speech sounds with movements of the lips. Obviously, it's beyond the scope of the beginner to show all the lip movements (even the professionals don't do it). But you can simulate key sounds and provide accessory cutouts of the mouth to use with them (Figure 64). See more about this in Chapter 15, which deals with sound tracks and lip-sync.

Fig. 63 Speech balloons can be popped on and off the screen in a cutout film that does not have audible dialogue.

Fig. 64 For cutout animation with audible dialogue, make a set of accessory mouth shapes for each speaking character.

11

ANIMATING ON CELS

Perhaps this chapter should have appeared near the front of this book. But that would be like telling a joke with the punch line first.

Why? Because the more sophisticated cel technique, the bailiwick of cartoon animation, is the *pièce de résistance* of the entire animation menu. It is certainly the most entertaining and memorable. That's why you see more cel production on television and movie screens than any other type of animation.

The term *cartoon* used here means all animated drawings inked and painted on transparent acetate cels, then photographed. This includes the beautifully executed "realistic" art seen in some of the feature-length animated films. You don't have to deal solely with comic characters when doing animation, especially if you have a talent for fine art. However, you will find that the simple, well-defined lines of cartoons are ideally suited to cel animation.

So, how do you go about getting cartoon action onto a reel of film?

Some of the steps have already been discussed in earlier chapters, because many of the tools and techniques apply to all or several types of animation. Before getting into cel animation, however, it is suggested that you reread Chapter 7, particularly the sections about animation stands and establishing a peg system for registering your animation drawings. A familiarity with the use of register pegs is of top priority. You can work with your camera mounted on a tripod in lieu of an animation stand. But you must, repeat must, have a baseboard equipped with register pegs if you are to deal accurately with dozens and dozens of animation cels. Without accurate positioning, you'll wind up with a film that looks like an unmade bed.

As you have already learned in Chapter 7, you can buy peg bars and pre-punched cels and animation paper. Or you can devise your own economical system, using the variety of materials for pegs and the hole-punching systems described in that chapter. Punched sheets of thin typewriter paper will serve for making basic drawings. The important thing is to equip both your drawing board and the baseboard of your animation stand (one board can serve for both) with register pegs before you start drawing.

It's also advisable to make sure you have an adequate supply of punched drawing paper and cels on hand. So, you must pre-plan your film.

Yes, yes, we've harped on pre-planning before. And at the risk of being a bore, we'll probably bring it up again. But don't knock this necessary navigational device. As you know by now, you will probably need a minimum of about 12 drawings for every second of your film. And even a run-of-the-mill action like a woman walking requires at least two layers of cels in every frame you photograph. Add another layer or two if the action is more complicated. Add a background. Add all that up and remember that you have to multiply by 60 to get a full minute of film — and you'll see why some pre-planning and pre-stocking are called for.

You can also see why it would probably be best to limit your debut in cel animation to a one-minute film. (But if you are really eager to take a full plunge, instead of just getting your feet wet, a Super 8 cartridge runs 3 minutes and 20 seconds, or 3,600 frames. That's a pretty deep plunge for your first time off the low board.)

MATERIALS FOR CEL ANIMATION

The animation stands, peg systems, lighting, and cameras discussed in Chapter 7 can be used in one or more of the various animation production techniques. Cel animation uses them all, and has some special needs as well.

Cels

These clear plastic sheets are made of acetate, usually 5 mils thick. A uniform set of holes is punched along the top margin of each cel. The holes must, of course, match and fit snugly over the register pegs in your drawing board and the baseboard of your animation stand.

Standard cels often used by professional animators are 10" x 12" (25 x 30 cm). Larger cels are often used in panning and for moving backgrounds. You don't have to work on professional-size cels, however. In fact, you can do very well with similar sheets of, say 8 ½" x 11" (21.6 x 28 cm) that you fashion yourself. This will save money; here are two suggestions for stretching your budget:

- Purchase clear acetate file folders at a stationery store. These already have a number of holes punched in them, so you will have to devise register pegs to match. Cut them in half and make two cels from each folder.

- Purchase large sheets or rolls of clear acetate at an art supply store and cut cels in the desired size. Use a three-hole office punch to make the register holes.

When buying clear acetate, specify either the treated or untreated kind, according to how much you are willing to spend. The treated acetate, which usually costs approximately 20 percent more than the untreated sheets, is coated with a special material so that inks, dyes, and paints will readily adhere to it without "creeping" and "beading."

Some drawing media will not easily adhere to untreated acetate. This

---

A SHOPPING LIST OF CEL ANIMATION "EXTRAS"

- A liquid "base," which, when mixed with opaque ink or paint, produces a transparent color for painting shadows and other tonal effects

- Tints for increasing or decreasing the intensity of colors in successive layers of cels

- Pre-punched drawing paper to fit standard peg bars

- Pre-punched tracing paper to fit standard peg bars

- Punched and unpunched sheets or rolls of Bristol paper for making panoramic backgrounds for panning or moving (you can get up to 750 feet [23 meters] in a roll)

- Clear or frosted animation cels more than a yard (0.9 meter) wide or in 100-foot (30-meter) rolls

- Colored animation cels

- Colored blanks for backgrounds

- Storyboard pads for roughing in the action

- Pads of printed exposure sheets (dope sheets) for plotting camera procedures

- Printed field guides to aid in layout and camera work

- Time-footage computing charts for 16mm and 35mm film

- Register hole punchers

- Peg hole reinforcements

- Strips of punched peg holes to attach to unpunched artwork

- Light cotton "inking gloves" to prevent fingerprints on cels

- Anti-static fluid and cloths for cleaning cels

- Assorted pens, pen-holders, brushes

- Transfer paper that works like carbon paper, with less mess

- Stopwatches that measure both seconds and film footage

- Rulers with holes that fit over register pegs

- Pegged inking boards

- Light boxes

- Automated animation stands

- Pressure-sensitive alphabets for titling

- And (wouldn't you know!) sheets of rub-on cartoon heads, hair, eyes, ears, noses, mouths, and hands problem can often be overcome if the acetate is given a light coating of workable fixative spray. Too much spray, however, will cause a milky film on the cell and reduce the clarity of the lines and colors on underlying cels and backgrounds. For the same reason, it's not a good idea to use frosted acetate for cels.

Drawing Paper

Unless you have the courage and skill to draw directly on the cels, you'll need to do preliminary sketches on paper. As might be surmised, a so-called animation drawing paper is sold for this purpose. It is really nothing more than a good quality bond paper with a degree of transparency, cut to the dimensions that professional animators use and perforated for registering. Any semi-transparent typewriter paper you can obtain, the cheaper the better, will suit your purpose — providing it has a good surface for making pencil drawings. These drawings are for working out the details of your animation movements. Once drawn, they can be traced in ink on cels.

Also, a pad or punched sheets of tracing vellum will often prove handy to have available for detailed tracings or for working out complex arrangements within the film frame.

Inks, Paints, and Dyes

At the outset, ordinary opaque India ink will do for drawing your characters on cels. (Black is the accepted color for this, but you needn't limit yourself to it.) Later on you can graduate to the inks formulated especially for work on animation cels. They're available in containers of up to a gallon (3.8 liters)!

Several transparent dyes and opaque paints in a broad spectrum of colors also are available for professional and amateur animators. For now, you may be just as happy and creative with some old standbys like poster colors and house paints. The first, tempera and gouache paints, can be made to adhere to untreated acetate cels if you mix a drop or two of laundry detergent with them. They're penny pinchers, too, because they can be washed off later on and the cels used again.

Acrylic paints and latex house paints will also work (when slightly watered down). The color range of latex is limited, but you can extend your palette by mixing in watercolor pigments from the tube.

The brilliantly colored lacquers found in small jars in hobby supply stores can be used for special effects. Beware of their tendency to reflect light from their glossy surfaces.

Transparent Colors

Thus far, we've talked principally about opaque inks and paints, the normal items for painting on animation cels. You may also want to use some transparent colors when preparing backgrounds, overlays, and cutouts. Prominent among the useful transparent colors are Dr. Martin's dyes and ordinary watercolors. However, watercolor will stick only to treated acetate, if you should want to paint on cels.

Waterproof or permanent felt markers with broad nibs are good when transparent colors are desired.

Other Media

Crayons, litho pencils, and china markers can be used to obtain bold and unusual line effects. When using them, as well as when using the felt markers, guard against smears and smudges. Also, if left too long under the heat of photoflood lamps, crayons and marker lines that contain wax will melt and spread.

Shopping List

There's still a whole big animation supermarket to be explored. Add a few extra sheets of paper for preliminary sketches and charting, and you can do very nicely with the animation materials mentioned above. You can even do with less. But as you become more adept, you may want to investigate additional animation and art materials. (See the "Shopping List" box on page 84.) They are the extras that animators use to improve speed and expand their capabilities.

A SAMPLE EXERCISE

Let's assume, for a beginning exercise, that you are to produce cel animation of approximately one minute duration. For reasons of economy, you will:

- Use a Super 8 camera

- Film in color

- And, though this first effort will not have oral dialogue, you will use film with a sound track so that music and possibly some sound effects can be added later on.

This means you will plan and shoot your film for projection at a speed of 24 fps.

CHECKLIST OF PROCEDURE

Perhaps the easiest way to get the whole project organized in your mind is to prepare and follow a checklist. Such a list is shown on page 87 and tells the things you will need to do.

BEFORE FILMING

The first three items on the checklist have been pretty much gone into in earlier chapters. However, it is worthwhile dropping a reminder that when developing characters, you should make them as simple as possible. You can use versions of the ready-made characters shown in previous chapters. But you'll get more pleasure and satisfaction in creating your own characters.

Somebody has to be first off the mark, so, for the purpose of demonstration, we will use a few frames showing a little medieval page (Figure 65) taken from a film titled *Mother Told Me There Would be Knights Like This*.

Using this, we can proceed with fuller explanations of the other items on the checklist.

STORYBOARD

Your story idea and the characters that people it get together for the first time in a *storyboard* — a series of small sketches that are a form of pictorial shorthand (Figure 66). They should be roughed in as soon as possible, because they will give you a capsule visual impression of how your animation will appear. A storyboard is like a page from a comic book. It doesn't show every movement that will appear in your film, but it does provide glimpses of key frames as the action progresses.

You don't have to take too much care sketching your storyboard. But do spend enough time with its contents to establish camera fields, the size and position of characters within the frames, whether panning or background movements will be needed, and other pertinent information. Make notes of each decision under the pictures, including your estimates of the time each segment will require.

Storyboarding is a good time to take another leaf from the comic books and consider zooms. As was mentioned in the chapter on cutout animation, comic-strip artists capture and hold viewer interest by switching back and forth from long views of a scene to extreme close-ups, to medium shots, and so on.

This movement in and out is especially helpful for improving ccl animation. Try it in yours.

Pads of blank storyboards can be purchased at art supply stores. But since you are probably the only person to see and use this capsule visualization of your first film, you can easily make your own. Be sure to draw the rectangular frames in the same proportion as the frames on the film you are using. Figure 66 shows a reduced segment of the original storyboard for *Mother Told Me There Would be Knights Like This*, which was shot on Super 8 film. Thus, the sketched frames of the storyboard were approximately 4" x 3" (10 x 8 cm) in size.

TIMING

With storyboard in hand, you are now ready to work out the timing of each action. For example, how long does it take the page to carry the wine cask to his irascible boss, the knight? When the knight finally is in the saddle, how fast should the horse move and for how long? Even how long does it take a bead of sweat to run down the page's brow?

It all adds up. Each little detail should be timed and added to a cumulative total. In this way you can determine the overall running time of the film as it is depicted on the storyboard. If it proves to be longer or shorter than you had anticipated, you must make adjustments in the pace of the film, perhaps even eliminating or inserting a scene. Ideally, you will want your story to move along at a brisk pace in keeping with the lively nature of cartoon animation. One of the most common faults of amateur animation is that it moves too slowly.

The task of timing is further complicated by the fact that some motions overlap one another within the total time segments. While the chore

of boosting the knight into the saddle was going on, the animator also had to time the fall of perspiration popping from the page's head (see close-up of perspiring page in the storyboard). These little simultaneous actions do not add to the overall length of the film, but they must be reckoned with just the same.

Don't forget the film title! The showing of the title, some film credits (don't be modest), and a final THE END all require several seconds — perhaps as many as 300 frames in all — and should be included in your overall calculations.

Most do-it-yourself animators develop the combined skill of working out the timing of actions as they are roughed in on a storyboard. You must visualize, either in your mind or on paper, the key positions of a movement (they're often called *extremes*) and determine how long it should take to move from one extreme to the next. Thus, you may find that, in order to determine the timing of a scene, you will get well into the task of establishing key drawings (extremes) for your animation.

ESTIMATING THE NUMBER OF DRAWINGS

If that is the easiest way for you to work, by all means go to it. But at some point along the way you will have to take an accounting for the purpose of knowing how many drawings and how many cels you will ultimately need to produce the film. Each movement must be timed to determine the number of frames needed to show it (at the rate of 24 fps). Each segment of each movement, including simultaneous movements, must be broken down and timed. For example, a character's head may turn while he or she is walking and thus, the head, body, and legs, perhaps the arms as well, will be drawn on separate sheets.

When a grand total of required drawings is determined (and here's the good news), you can reduce it by half, because you will probably film your animation on twos — that is, shoot each frame twice before changing cels. In some instances you may shoot on threes or fours, when a slower pace is in order.

Remember that all your animation drawings and segments of drawings must be transferred to acetate cels. Then, do your arithmetic well and make certain you have sufficient supplies of drawing paper and cels on hand and that each sheet is perforated to fit snugly on your register pegs.

KEY DRAWINGS

Now begins the fascination of creating a jigsaw of moving bits and pieces, then fitting them together to project a logical and smooth-flowing motion. Consider, as an example, a bit of action by the medieval page in the storyboard. The poor little guy does a great deal of walking in this film, usually toting a wine cask for his boss, so that's what we'll show him doing.

Since walking is a fairly straight-forward action, the extremes of the movement, it would seem, should be the beginning of the first step and the end of the last one. That's true as the complete stroll is viewed on the screen. But we can draw the page taking only one full stride (Figure 67) and use the drawings as a cycle to be repeated again and again as he plods his weary way. The first extreme of the cycle is the page with the cask on his shoulder and one foot slightly raised as he starts the stride. The other extreme is at the end of the stride. There are only two in-betweens.

Study the cels used in the striding action and you will note they include a key drawing and what we will call *movement drawings*. The first is that part of the page's body that is repeated without change. His head, torso, and the arm clasping the wine cask make up the key drawing. The four positions of the legs are movement drawings. The page's near arm must also be shown as movement drawings. It swings back and forth as he walks.

This breaking down of the action into separate parts and drawing only those that move is called limited animation. You can see unlimited limited animation any Saturday morning on television.

IN-BETWEENING

In-betweens, the drawings for intermediate positions between the extremes of an action, are necessary in nearly all movements — though we have reduced the number to only two for the page's stride. You probably can animate the walk of any character you create by adapting the extremes and in-betweens shown in Figures 62 and 67.

Detailed instructions for creating a walk cycle are also provided in the previous chapter. That example is

---

CEL ANIMATION CHECKLIST OF PROCEDURE

BEFORE FILMING

Provide a lighted animation stand of some sort.

Provide a register peg system for drawing board and baseboard.

Plan your story/message and develop the characters.

Prepare a rough storyboard.

Time action(s) in each scene.

Estimate number and obtain drawing paper and cels.

Prepare key drawings on punched paper.

Prepare in-between drawings on punched paper.

Trace all drawings in ink on punched cels.

Paint color and white-ins on backs of cels.

Draw and color background(s) on punched illustration paper.

Prepare final detailed dope sheet of number and sequence of cels to be photographed.

SHOOTING THE FILM

Secure camera in stand. Adjust and check field of vision and focus.

Check lights and exposure setting. Make certain there are no reflections in field of vision.

Check frame counter and single-frame exposure release.

Expose 12 or more blank frames to serve as a "buffer zone" when splicing or adding leader.

Place background, first set of cels, and glass platen in position and begin single-frame exposures.

Check off each frame on the dope sheet immediately after it is exposed.

When last frame has been shot, expose a dozen more blank frames on the tail end of your film.

for animating cutouts and is for a camera field of about 14 inches (36cm) in width. In cel animation, it is suggested that you work on a 12-inch (30.5cm) field or smaller, but you can easily adapt the instructions for cutouts to this smaller size. Instead of drawing and cutting out four sets of legs, simply draw them as in-betweens on animation paper, then trace them onto cels.

Follow the same procedure for drawing extremes and in-betweens for the movement of the page's (or your character's) arm. Take a tip from nature and note that a walking person's arms swing back and forth at approximately the same rate that his or her legs are moving. To maintain balance, the right arm swings forward with the left leg as the left arm and right leg are trailing and vice versa. Watch a walking or jogging person in action and copy this body-balancing act in your animation drawings.

One of Sir Isaac Newton's laws of motion can give you a technical explanation for all this swinging back and forth. But what it boils down to

is this: if you draw a walk cycle and show the leg movements in four stages, the arm movements should likewise be in four stages.

All key drawings and in-betweens should be drawn on punched paper held in position on your drawing board by register pegs. Once the key drawing is sketched in and cleaned up to sharpen the lines, register a clean sheet of paper over it and draw the first stage of the arm and leg movement in exact position. Place another sheet of paper on the pegs and draw the second stage of the motion. And so on.

It is at this point that you will begin to appreciate the semi-transparent quality of the animation paper, because each set of legs must be precisely joined to the key drawing of the body. The arm must always swing from the same point at the shoulder. If your paper is not transparent enough for clear positioning of your drawings, you will have to devise a register peg system on a light box or with some other method of backlighting.

NUMBERS, PLEASE

For the sake of maintaining your sanity, be sure to identify each drawing as you complete it. Otherwise, one or two may go astray and throw your entire sequence of motion into disarray. The standard method for keeping track of the drawings (and subsequently the cels traced from them) is to give capital letters to each cel layer that will appear under the camera, and give numerals to the succession of drawings that will be used in the same *cel level*.

In our example, there are only two cel levels. The key drawing will be on Level A and the movement drawings will be placed on top of it, on Level B. Thus the key drawing (and later the cel) should be marked A1 in one of its corners out of the camera field. The four movement cels that go on top of it one at a time would be marked B1, B2, B3, and B4.

Often, when animating intricate movements you will need more than two cel levels in each frame — as many as five in some cases, but don't use more than five, the practical limit. You will be handling the cels many times under the camera, so think ahead when numbering them to make the frame changes as easy as possible. Number the cels so that the most frequently changed ones will be in the upper levels and you can avoid removing the whole stack from the register pegs every time you change the in-betweens of a movement.

TRACING ON CELS

After all your many animation drawings are made on paper, after they are checked and cleaned up, settle yourself comfortably for the long and often humdrum task of tracing (*inking*) them onto cels. Someday you may become skilled enough to do some of your drawing directly on

Fig. 65 *The little page, star of* Mother Told Me There Would Be Knights Like This.

Fig. 66 Four frames from a storyboard. These can be roughly sketched but should give some indication of camera fields, types of backgrounds, special effects, and more.

cels without making preliminary drawings, but for now let's play it safe.

Obviously, tracing is less creative and pleasurable than making the original drawings. But this portion of the animation production routine requires skill and concentration. Don't treat it lightly.

Ideally, the inking is done on a light box equipped with register pegs, but this is not an absolute necessity. The outline only is traced (usually in black) on the top surface of the cel. The tracing pen preferred by many animators is a Rapidograph or an equivalent technical pen. These are available with an assortment of nibs for drawing lines of various thicknesses. The Rapidograph No. 3 nib makes a good, easily visible line for animation — neither too thick nor too thin.

Here's how the inking procedure might go:

1. Place a key animation drawing on the pegs of your light box or drawing board and register a blank cel over it.

2. Make sure the cel is free of dirt, grease, and fingerprints. (Wearing cotton film-editing gloves is recommended at this stage.)

If fingerprints or oil smears from your hands do get onto the cel, wipe them away with a dab of absorbent cotton dampened with a mild cleaning solvent or rubber cement thinner.

3. Trace over the *exact* lines of the animation drawing underneath the cel. This is no time to be smitten by creative inspiration or attempts to "improve" the state of your art. If you want to make changes, make a new set of animation drawings, then trace them.

4. Keep a small sponge dampened with water or a clean, damp rag

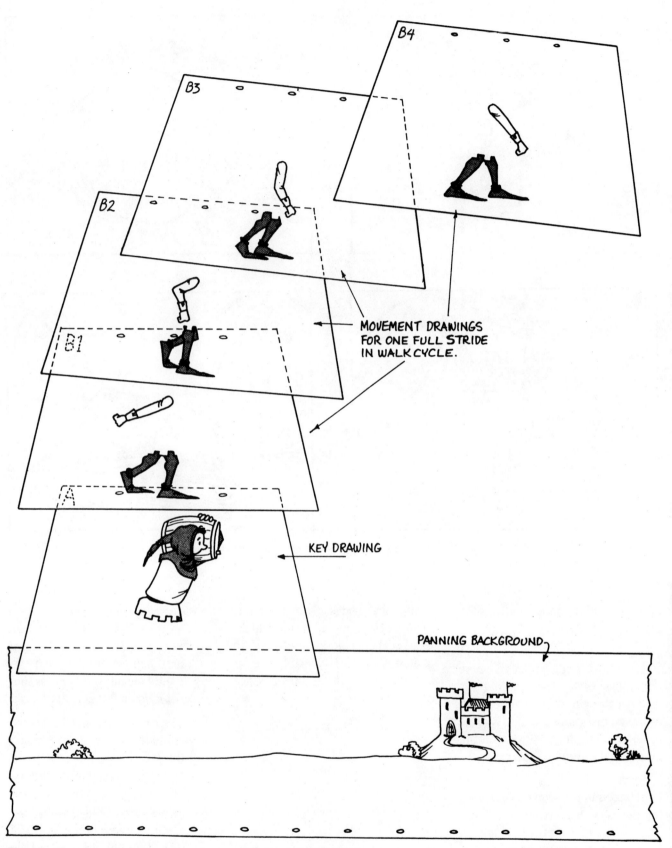

B4

B3

B2

B1

A

MOVEMENT DRAWINGS
FOR ONE FULL STRIDE
IN WALK CYCLE.

KEY DRAWING

PANNING BACKGROUND

Fig. 67 *The elements of a walk cycle on cels. The background pans east-west with a stationary key drawing (the page's torso) on top of it. The movement cels (in-betweens) are alternately placed on the key drawing and photographed.*

close by so that mistakes, blots, and stray lines can be wiped off while the ink is still wet.

5. Number the cel before taking it from the register pegs. Some animators put the number between the register holes instead of in the corner of the sheet.

6. When all the cels are inked (you'll have quite a stack, even for a one-minute film), carefully check them to make sure none has been omitted and that the inked lines are sharp and solid. If you have purchased pre-punched animation cels, they probably arrived with thin sheets of tissue separating them. It's a good idea to continue using these protective separation sheets while sorting, stacking, and later storing your inked and opaqued cels.

OPAQUING AND WHITING-IN

Now we go to the flip side of the cels. With some few exceptions, the color and the *whiting-in* that you apply to the cels should be painted on the reverse side of that on which you inked the outlines of the figures (Figure 68). This will prevent weakening or otherwise spoiling the ink lines. Another advantage is that, by painting on the back side, you can overlap the color onto the inked outlines to avoid leaving transparent gaps around the edges. Should you accidentally brush color or opaque white beyond the outline, it's easy enough to remove the excess without harming the outline on the other side of the cel.

As was mentioned elsewhere, professional cel vinyl paints are available specifically for the job of opaquing. Acrylic paints will also serve, and for the amateur, latex house paints and poster colors will do. The latter will need a touch of

Fig. 68 *Front and back of an inked animation cel showing the opaque color painted on the reverse side.*

detergent mixed in to keep the paint from flaking off the cels.

Felt markers and Dr. Martin's dyes can also be used for coloring. But because of their transparency, their use is limited to special tones and effects. In most cases you will have to use opaque paints, and you will

have to make certain they are applied in even, opaque layers so that lines of the background or other objects underneath your animated characters will not show through. For example, the area of a moving arm must be painted with opaque paint so the outlines of the body underneath will not show through it.

As in inking, make sure your cels are perfectly clean and grease-free before opaquing. Don't try to paint all the colors and complete one cel at a time. Rather, treat them like an assembly line, painting a single color on every cel where it is called for, then going back to the first cel and starting over with the next color.

If you are not using standard colors, be sure to mix enough of each color to do the entire set of cels. It is difficult to match a mixed color if you run short of it halfway through the painting. If you do have to mix and match, remember to compare dry paint with dry paint to match the color. Wet paint reflects more light than dry and appears more intense.

When all the opaquing is completed, check the cels again while you have the colors handy for touching-up and corrections.

BACKGROUNDS — STATIONARY OR MOVING?

There are three basic types of backgrounds in non-professional cel animation: (1) stationary, (2) moving, and (3) blank background.

You may wish to design the background or backgrounds of your film *before* making the drawings of your characters. Some animators find that having the background already drawn gives them a "stage" on which to visualize the players, making it easier to plot their proportions and movements. This is particularly true when the action is in some way related to objects in the background or to its perspective.

The following chapter deals with backgrounds in detail. But whether you actually draw yours first or last, you will have to make an early decision about your background, because it will determine to some extent the

method of preparing your animation drawings and how many you will have to draw. If, for example, you elect to have a moving background, one that is drawn or painted on a long strip of paper that is moved to the right or left to simulate the progress of your characters, you will need fewer key drawings than you would for a moving figure on a stationary background, because the key drawing remains in one spot as the background moves along behind it.

The most common example of this is again the animation of a walking figure. The figure remains stationary (except for the moving legs and arms) in the center of the camera field, and the background moves past, giving the illusion that it is the figure that is making tracks down the garden path.

On the other hand, if you want to let your figure do the walking on a stationary background, you must devise a way to move him or her literally across the camera field. This can be done in two ways:

1. Re-ink the entire figure at each stage of the leg movements, changing the position of the figure on the cel each time to move it progressively across the camera field. Once the figure reaches the extreme right or left side of the frame, you must cut to another scene or have a very good reason for his walking out of the picture.

2. Draw only the key drawing and movement drawings for a walk cycle on separate cels as described earlier. But use extra length cels so that they can be moved from side to side to propel the walking figure across the camera's field of vision.

Don't think you can duck any of these problems by using a plain background. A blank area is the same as

a stationary background, and you should use either of the two procedures described immediately above, making your figures literally move across the screen. To hold a walking figure too long in center screen on a blank background gives the impression that he or she is simply marking time in one spot and going nowhere. It's OK for treading grapes but not for strolling.

Does all this seem complicated? It really isn't. A more detailed (and head-clearing) explanation of animating on both stationary and moving backgrounds will be gone into in the next chapter. Meanwhile, back at the drawing board, let's look at the *dope sheet*.

THE DOPE SHEET

The last thing on your checklist before actual filming is a very important step. It is to prepare a frame-by-frame shooting schedule for the camera. This is called a dope sheet or, in nicer terms, an exposure sheet. "Dope sheet" is film jargon, but some claim it derives from the fact that you're a dope if you don't use one. It brings order out of chaos.

It could indeed be chaos, because by this time you will have inked and painted several hundred animation cels. The function of the dope sheet is to list, one frame at a time, the order in which the cels will be under the camera for photographing and how many times, along with additional directions for backgrounds and camera movements.

An equally important feature of the dope sheet is that, when compiling it, you can finalize in detail the timing of each action in the film, and each simultaneous or overlapping motion. Previously, when drawing your storyboard, you estimated the timing for various actions and determined the length of your film. You may have decided, for example, that the leaping of a cat should take three seconds. But since a cat doesn't travel at the same rate of speed from start to finish, it is on the dope sheet that you work out and record the details of the cat's slow start, its acceleration, and so on. This will determine whether you shoot a certain group of cels for one frame only, or for two, three, or more frames. (This is the "slowing in" and "slowing out" mentioned in Chapter 9.)

When compiling an animation dope sheet, you are in effect doing in advance what producers of live action movies do in the film editing and cutting room.

You can buy printed exposure (dope) sheets used by professionals, but they're a shade on the complicated side. Make your own simply by drawing vertical column rules on ruled paper and labeling the columns (Figure 69).

The left-hand column should be labeled FRAME and should be numbered 1, 2, 3, and so on through the several hundreds of frames you will photograph for the film. The next five columns (no more, please) are for indicating the cel levels for each frame. Label them A through E, or by whatever designation you have been marking your cel levels as you inked them. A column should be provided labeled BACKGROUND, so that you can record instructions for movement or changes in backgrounds. An important final column, headed CAMERA, should be used for instructions such as "fade in," "start zoom," and so on.

An optional column can provide space for a brief description of the action — "ball rolling," "girl shouting," "man biting dog." And if you plan to add music or sound effects to your film, leave some space at the right of the dope sheet for additional

frame-by-frame instructions for dubbing in sound later.

SHOOTING THE FILM

One thing not mentioned before in regard to designing or arranging your animation stand (Chapter 7) is the element of physical fatigue involved in exposing even a minute of film one frame at a time. It is a lengthy and often monotonous repetition of hand, arm, back, and head motions. You may not think that lifting a sheet of acetate off register pegs takes much energy, but by the time you've done it 473 or 796 times, you'll wonder how the lead weights got into your arms.

One way to lick the problem is to take periodic rests. But the better way is to attack it at its source and avoid undue stretching and bending.

TITLE:							SHEET No. ___	
SCENE:							FPS ___	

ACTION	FRAME No.	CEL NUMBER					BACKGROUND	CAMERA
		A	B	C	D	E		
	1							
	2							
	3							
	4							
	5							
	6							
	7							
	8							
	9							
	10							
	11							
	12							
	13							
	14							
	15							
	16							
	17							
	18							
	19							
	20							
	21							
	22							
	23							
	24							
	25							
	26							

Fig. 69 A dope sheet for basic cel animation. Make one of your own, leaving the "Frame No." column blank, and photocopy it to provide plenty of copies. Also, see Figure 113 for a dope sheet with a column for sound.

CAMERA COUNT-DOWN

1. WIPE CAMERA LENS CLEAN
2. WIND CAMERA
3. ADJUST FOR LIGHT, FOCUS, FILM
4. SET FOR SINGLE-FRAMING
5. LIGHTS ON
6. CHECK ARTWORK FOR POSITION
7. CHECK ARTWORK FOR SHADOWS
8. HANDS OUT OF WAY?
   SHOOT!

Fig. 70 *A camera countdown list. Keep one handy as a pre-flight check before shooting.*

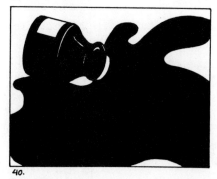

Fig. 71 *Four frames from an add-on sequence. If the bottle is drawn on paper and fastened to the baseboard, the spread of the ink can be accomplished under the camera by adding a bit more ink after each exposure.*

Arrange, if possible, to be comfortably seated while making the exposures. And, whether you are seated or standing, be sure to have your stack of prepared cels within easy reach, your dope sheet where you can reach it, and ample space for stacked used cels after they have been shot. Remember that in shooting cycles, some of your cels will be handled again and again and should be kept within reach — and in the correct order.

THE BUDDY SYSTEM

You may be a loner who prefers to fly solo during your creative efforts. But for this less creative phase of animation, consider the possible advantage of getting a friend to join the team — for fun and for efficiency. One person can operate the camera while the other reads the dope sheet and manipulates the cels.

USING THE CHECKLIST

Another thing to remember is that shooting your film frame-by-frame is basically a mechanical routine and, therefore, tedious. When things become boring, we tend to lose interest in the routine and run the risk of neglecting details, botching the job. That's why it's wise to make a checklist (Figure 70) and keep it handy. Do a pre-flight check as an airline pilot does each time you man your camera.

A checklist like this could include even more details, some of them almost insulting when mentioned. For instance, did you load the camera? And did you wind the camera? You'd be surprised how many people forget to. Here are some more strings to tie on your finger.

- Use film recommended for indoors, and follow the manufacturer's instructions.

- Always use a cable release for tripping the shutter during single-frame shooting to avoid jiggling the camera.

- To maintain uniform clarity and color, keep the same number of cels under the camera when shooting every frame. Find the sequence that requires the most cel levels and let that be the standard number throughout the film. If, for example, it is four levels, in frames that require fewer than four cels insert a blank cel or cels on top to maintain the uniform number.

• When all is in place for shooting a frame (background, cels, and glass platen), check for shadows and reflections. Some professionals and advanced amateurs attach polarizing filters to their flood-lamps to reduce reflections.

• Hands up! Be sure they're out of the camera field before you click the shutter.

• The checklist item about marking off each frame on the dope sheet immediately after it is exposed is worth repeating. Until you've started the supposedly steady routine of shooting, you'll never know how many unforeseen distractions can arise. A ringing doorbell, a blown fuse ... and when you come back to the animation stand you'll be wondering did you or did you not expose a frame of the cels lying there. If you've kept your dope sheet up to date, meaning each frame checked off, you can tell at a glance. Put a tick beside the frame number or circle it when the frame is exposed. Do it immediately.

• Likewise, don't trust your memory during longer intervals in the shooting routine. When you knock off for the day, jot down the camera settings, frame counter number, camera field, and other pertinent information so that you can check them when you resume work.

This is as good a time as any to remind you that the edges of the cel register holes are not indestructible. Care should be taken when putting cels on or removing them from the pegs so that the holes will not be-

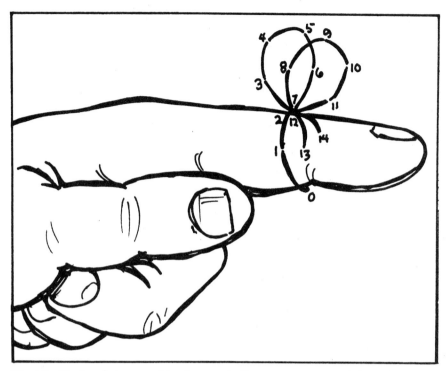

Fig. 72 Each number on this diagram indicates a segment of the string to be added following exposure of two frames.

come ragged and enlarged. Loose-fitting cels cause wobbly images on the screen. This care should begin when the cels are inked.

ADDING, SUBTRACTING, AND POP-ONS

In the earlier chapter about drawing directly on film without using a camera, some mention was made of add-on animation in which a figure or design grows before your eyes on the screen. Reverse the process and a projected image disappears bit by bit. It's great fun when drawing on film, and it's even more fun — providing many imaginative possibilities — when adapted for cel animation.

Simply stated, you start with an image in mind, a spilled bottle of ink, for example (Figure 71). You show the tipped bottle and a bit of ink that has spilled from it. Then you keep adding a bit more ink on the cel as you shoot succeeding frames until

the ink has become a wide, wavy line running out of the frame or perhaps a spreading blob that eventually blanks out the screen. This add-on animation is especially helpful in titling the films. Words and whole phrases seem to write themselves.

DRAWING ON THE STAND

You can do delightful but simple add-on animation right on the animation stand without any preliminary sketches. Register a plain sheet of paper on the baseboard pegs. Draw the first small portion of your design and expose one or two frames in the camera. Add the next small unit of your drawing and shoot another one or two frames. Repeat this routine until your drawing is completed.

For more intricate add-on animation, and for better control of the quality of your design, it is best to make a preliminary sketch to be used as a guide (Figure 72). Mark and number the portions of the sketch in

Fig. 73 *Two frames from an animated film,* The Flight of the Left Wing Red Bird. *Five birds were popped onto the screen one at a time.*

the order that they will be added to the cel. Put this reference sketch on the animation stand pegs with a blank cel over it and ink the first unit. Slide a blank sheet of paper between the sketch and the cel and shoot the desired number of frames. Remove the blank sheet and ink the next unit on the reference sketch. Re-insert the blank. Ink the next — ta-dum — ta-dum — ta-dum —

SUBTRACTING

Just as you can add bits and pieces on the screen, you can also make them disappear. To do this, draw a growing figure or design as if you were doing add-on animation, but draw and photograph each frame *upside down.* When the film has been processed, reverse the ends so the front becomes the tail, and voilá, you have a disappearing act.

Unless the disappearing picture is your entire film, which is unlikely, you will have to do a bit of splicing to fit it into the "normal" film.

POP-ONS

A variation on the add-on theme is to add complete units, *pop-ons,* sud-

denly to your design. They literally pop onto the screen without warning. You can add them at random, like the helter-skelter building of a jigsaw puzzle. Or you can add them in a controlled sequence (Figure 73).

The pop-on technique is useful in silent animation to suddenly add and remove speech words or a thought balloon above a character's head. In order for the audience to read and understand the dialogue, pop-on balloons should be left on the screen a little bit longer than the time it would take to say the words in balloons. A two-word statement, for example, takes about one second. So pop on the words and leave them there for 24 to 30 frames. This timing factor also applies when pop-ons are used in titling.

MAKING HEADS TURN

Cel animation and cutout animation are easiest to do when the characters are shown in profile or directly facing the camera. There's no problem of perspective on the figures themselves. But even in the simplest of films it is often desirable to get characters facing in one direction to turn

and face in another. The head and body must be rotated.

The easiest way to do that is to make a sudden cut from a profile to head-on or vice versa. This is great stuff for showing "double-takes," as any comic-strip artist will tell you. But in animation, too many quick cuts will cut your audience's interest in the film.

So do yourself a good turn and learn to rotate your figures at a normal speed. This will mean thinking of two-dimensional figures in the round. Heads, drawn as circles, should be imagined as globes; torsos as cylinders. To animate their turns, you will have to draw a number of in-betweens, but the result will be well worth the effort.

Let's make a head turn. It's easier than you think.

Assume that our subject is facing to one side (Figure 74) and you want his head to make a quarter-turn to face the camera. With the side and front views as extremes, a quarter-turn needs only two in-betweens. (These will be shot on twos to slow down the turn.)

Fig. 74

1.   2.   3.   4.

Figure 74 shows the order in which the heads are drawn. After the profile is completed, horizontal guidelines should be drawn from it through the other three globes. These will ensure that the eyes, noses, mouths, and ears will be at the same levels on all four heads. Use guidelines like this when you practice drawing in the round. Or do the drawings on graph paper.

Note that the ear on head No. 1 moves around to the edge of No. 3, and the other ear comes into view. (If you were to turn the man's whole body, you would move his shoulder and arm around in this way.) To help position the nose and other facial features on the in-betweens, it's also a good idea to draw a "longitude" line through each nose position (Figure 75). Cartoonists in all media often use such lines in their preliminary sketches as an aid in drawing heads at different angles. You should use them for preliminary sketches before transferring the heads to cels.

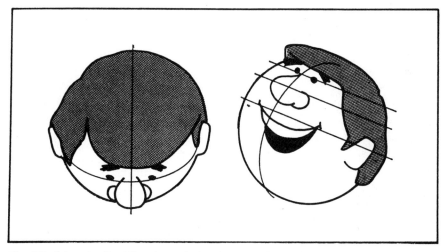

Fig. 75 *A longitudinal line through the nose can help when making drawings of a head turning in various directions.*

12

BACKGROUNDS AND FOREGROUNDS

It seems obvious, when you are planning an animated film, that it is a good idea to decide on the characters, the action, and the "stage" for the action — the background — all at the same time. And while we are being ever so wise, it is also good to remember the first law of animation — simplicity.

Just as it is wise to make your animated drawings as simple as possible to serve your purpose, it is also a good idea to be as sparing as possible with the backgrounds. Two general rules ought to apply:

HARMONY — Design your backgrounds to be compatible with the characters in them. If your animated figures are drawn or painted in a straightforward style, the background should also be fairly realistic. If, on the other hand, you are portraying abstract, exaggerated, or ultra-comic characters, your scenery should be in agreement in each case.

SUBORDINATENESS — No matter what style is used for your character-background combination, the background should not dominate and draw attention away from the action. Ideally, the background should be designed to contribute to the story by supporting the mood of the action and giving further explanation of what it is all about.

Thus, before starting to design a background scene for animation, you must ask yourself what contribution it is going to make to the total pro-

duction. And since it will make an unavoidable contribution, either by what it shows or doesn't show, it is best to plan this setting for your action at a very early stage. This may actually mean that you can eliminate backgrounds altogether from many of your sequences.

HISTORIC CYCLES

Whether you film your action in ornate settings or with no backgrounds at all, you're in good company, and there are ample historical precedents to back you up. In the very earliest days of commercial animation, in the work of French pioneer Emile Cohl, for example, no background scenes were shown. Each change of movement was drawn in its entirety on a separate sheet of paper. The technique of photographing the action on transparent sheets over separate backgrounds had not yet been devised.

With the development of cutouts, then cel animation, creative use of detailed and multi-planed moving backgrounds grew apace. Many cartoon animators resisted the temptation. But others, notably the Disney studio, dazzled viewers with colorfully extravagant settings for their equally vibrant characters.

With the growth of mass-produced cartoon animation for television, the cycle was reborn. Animators turned again to simple, often blank, backgrounds. But in the 1970s, spurred on by the development of the

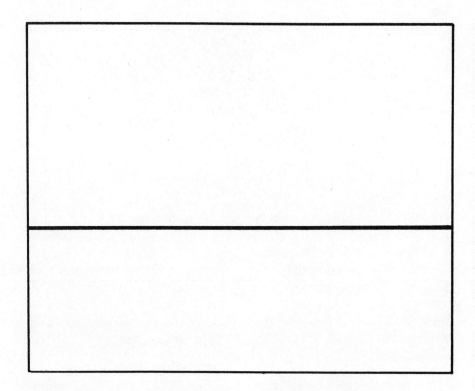

Fig. 76 *A single horizon line can set the scene for a wide variety of actions — indoors and out; on the ocean, prairie, or desert; in your neighborhood schoolyard.*

object on the screen without actually changing its dimensions. The bird seen against a distant horizon (Figure 77) is identical with the bird in the next frame. Yet, since the horizon line is lower, the impression when viewed on the screen will be that the camera is shooting upward at a relatively larger bird.

This visual principle can be applied to both stationary and moving backgrounds. It is particularly applicable in a very interesting animation technique called *over-the-camera* (Figure 78). Objects or characters appear to enter the field of vision over the top of the camera. The very low horizon line adds to the illusion that the camera rests on the floor and enhances the size of the moving figure.

rotoscoping technique (mentioned in Chapter 2), feature-length animated films were again being released with minutely detailed and realistic settings.

BASIC BACKGROUND DESIGN

In order to make a background work for you, you must consider it in relation to the characters or objects that will move in it. An example of this is the simplest of simple background drawings — nothing more than a single horizontal line (Figure 76) representing the horizon line of your scene of action. Depending on what you are portraying, that single line can be the separation of a floor and wall of a room, the horizon of an ocean, a prairie vista, the Sahara Desert, the edge of a table, and so on and on.

By moving the line up or down, you can give the impression of increasing or decreasing the size of an

TO PAN OR NOT TO PAN

You have a choice in our film planning to opt for either a stationary background or a moving one. The first

Fig. 77 *Positioning of the horizon line can create an optical illusion. Though the two chickens below are identical, the one standing in front of the low horizon will seem larger on the screen.*

Fig. 78 *In this example of over-the-camera animation, the perspective of the walls and doors gives the illusion of depth to the corridor. The low horizon line is particularly helpful in over-the-camera filming.*

is just what the term implies. It just lies there, setting the scene, while all the action takes place in front of it.

A moving background, on the other hand, is often called a *panning background*, because it is used to accomplish what a panning camera does. In both cases the illusion is that the viewer's eye is following a character or an object as it moves across a scene.

Note that the preceding sentence says "across a scene," not across the screen or frame. To achieve side-to-side movement (west-east or east-west) with a stationary background, you must literally move the object itself from left to right or right to left.

With a panning background, the object remains in a fixed place within the field of vision, and the background moves from side to side to simulate the object's progress.

Thus, your choice of backgrounds — stationary or moving — really depends on the nature of the action you are portraying. If the action takes place more or less in one place (two people talking and gesturing, a spider spinning a web, a frog hopping off a lily pad), you'll do very well and save some work with a stationary background. If getting about is called for (a walking man, the flight of a plane, the progress of a car or kangaroo), in most cases you'll save time and effort by using a movable

background to pan along behind the action.

Of course, you can use both techniques in one filmed segment. To visualize all this, look at Figure 79. The bird enters the frame from the left on a stable background. By inking a series of cels, each positioning the bird farther to the right, the animator manages to get the bird to mid-frame. That's doing it the hard way.

Now study Figure 80. Note that the airplane (which doesn't flap its wings) in this example is inked on an extra-wide cel. The cel can be moved to the right, and the animator needs to ink only one airplane. He can move it on out of the frame to the

101

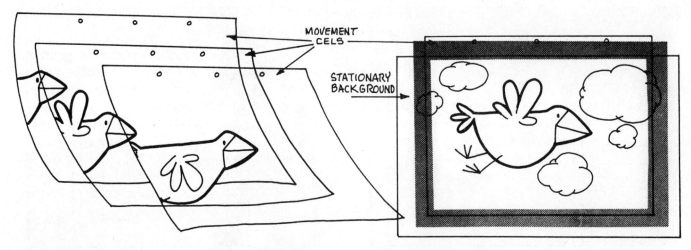

Fig. 79 *A series of separate action cels is needed to achieve the movement of a figure across a stationary background. More cels than those shown above will be needed to get the bird all the way across the frame.*

right. Or, since he has provided a moving background also, he can hold the airplane cel at mid-frame and move the background (to the left) to continue the flight. In this manner, the flight of the plane is limited only by the length of the background panning behind it.

Consider, in your mind's eye, how to translate the flight of the little airplane into the movement of a truck along a highway, a ship at sea, a boy on a speeding motorcycle. By adding animation cycles of moving legs or flapping wings, you can convert the method into a jogging person, running animal, or flying bird.

EXTENDING THE ACTION

The panoramic background shown in Figure 80 is a relatively short one. Thus the flight of the airplane on it would last a very few seconds. The duration of the flight, and the illusion of more distance, can be extended in two ways:

- One way is simply to draw or paint the background on a longer piece of paper. It is not uncommon for animators, both amateur

and professional, to render it a fraction of an inch at a time.

- Another way to extend the duration of an action is to use *panning cycles*. Start with a long, but manageable, panoramic background like the one in Figure 80. Once it has been moved its entire length across the camera's field of vision, move the background back to its original position and repeat the pan. This is called *jumping the pegs*. Some baseboards are equipped with *traveling peg bars*, which slide back and forth in a slot so that the background doesn't have to be lifted from the pegs.

Panning is a time- and material-saving trick that can be used extensively when the background is not repeated or when it does not have distinguishable "landmarks." Anonymous clouds, a line of roadside fence posts, an ocean horizon, for example, are especially useful as repeatable backgrounds. But be careful about using panning cycles with backgrounds containing recognizable objects and signs. If your film shows a woman walking along a street, your audience might become

amused or even confused if she passes the same drug store several times.

REGISTERING THE BACKGROUND

Naturally, you don't want your animated figures, over which you have labored long and carefully, to do their thing in front of a jiggly and jerky background. So you'll have to devise a method for holding the background in the correct positions and controlling its movements in panning cycles.

There are several ways of doing this, both professional and amateur. (And when we say professional, read *more expensive* or at least costing a bit more than do-it-yourself methods.)

DO-IT-YOURSELF REGISTERING

Until you graduate to "super amateur" or "lower-echelon professional," it's suggested that you try one or more of the ad hoc methods for registering panning backgrounds. They will work, provided you are careful enough when using them. They'll cost you nothing.

Method 1

Probably the most common do-it-yourself method for registering panning backgrounds is to create a groove into which the panoramic art can fit snugly as it slides back and forth. The so-called groove is made by gluing or taping two very thin strips of cardboard or wood horizontally across the baseboard (Figure 81). One strip is located at the top and outside of the field of vision and immediately below the pegs on which animation cels are registered. The other strip is placed below the field of vision.

Make sure the strips are exactly parallel and spaced so as to permit free lateral movement of the background artwork. They should be barely thicker than the background paper so that the glass platen you use will hold the background absolutely flat.

Method 2

Another way of holding panning backgrounds in register is by using vertical acetate strips taped over the panoramic artwork and outside the camera field (Figure 82). The background slides laterally beneath the strips. Four short pieces of thin cardboard are fastened above and below the artwork to serve as guides, just as the cardboard strips serve in the method previously described.

CEL MOVES RIGHT

BACKGROUND MOVES LEFT

Fig. 80 A panning cel and a panning background combine here to show the flight of an airplane. Since there are no moving parts on the plane, it was painted on an extra wide transparent cel (top drawing). This cel was panned west-east until the plane was at mid-frame (center). Then the cel was held stationary and the background panned east-west.

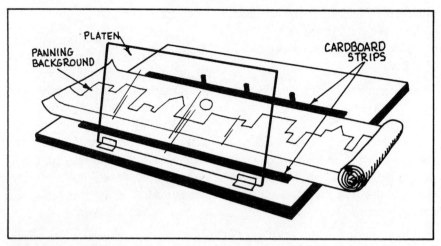

Fig. 81 *Thin strips of cardboard or wood can be fastened (temporarily) to the baseboard to guide the lateral movement of a background.*

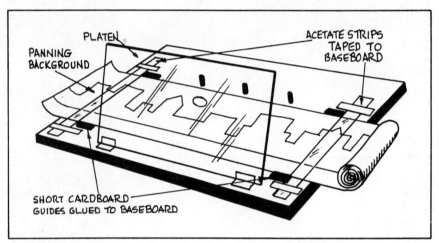

Fig. 82 *Acetate strips taped vertically on the baseboard will help guide the panning background, but small cardboard guides are needed to ensure accurate registration.*

Method 3

A third method is to install an additional set of register pegs near the bottom of the baseboard (Figure 83) and use these pegs to control panning movements of the background. You will have to put register holes all along the lower edge of the background. The extra pegs may also make it necessary for you to devise another way of hinging your platen to the baseboard, or it can be left loose.

TRAVELING PEG BAR

If you want to do a more sophisticated job of registering your back-grounds, short of investing in a highly technical and manipulative animation stand, a *traveling peg bar* is the answer. The bar holds three register pegs. By being fitted into a slot in the baseboard, instead of fastened to the board, the bar can slide from side to side (Figure 83), and the background doesn't have to be lifted from the pegs. Mark a ruler-like scale along the edge of the slot to guide you in measuring each movement of the sliding peg bar.

The trouble with such handy devices is that they usually work only with the aid of additional devices. If you opt for a traveling peg bar, you must also opt for matching register holes in your artwork.

You might, of course, be able to make a traveling peg bar of your own design, using round pegs that will accommodate the round register holes you can make with an office paper punch. But if you buy a traveling peg bar, it will have one round and two oblong pegs in it and you will have to arrange for punching your artwork with a matching trio of holes. You can buy a special hole puncher (either Acme or Oxberry). "But," as the man said, "they ain't cheap." You can also buy tapes of pre-punched register holes to attach to the edge of your artwork. But that costs money, too.

If you do install a traveling peg bar, put the slot at the *bottom* of the baseboard and outside the field of vision. Use this arrangement for backgrounds and leave the pegs near the top of the baseboard free for handling the action cels. Note that this means the register holes in your background will be punched at the bottom edge of the paper. Some animators install traveling peg bars at both the top and bottom of the baseboard so that panning can also be accomplished with cels on which characters and objects are inked. This was done with the airplane shown in Figure 80.

Caution: Before you cut a slot or slots in your baseboard, check your arrangement for hinging the glass platen in place. You may have to devise another setup, or unhinge the platen when the traveling peg bar is in use.

PAN CHART

Timing the movement of your panning background is important, because it will establish the speed at which your animated characters apparently are moving. The backgrounds behind an automobile or a perambulating penguin will pan at a different pace than one behind a strolling tortoise.

To gauge and regulate these movements, a *pan chart* should be marked along the edge of the background artwork (Figure 84). The markings are similar to those on a ruler but not always with standard spacing. With experience you will learn the most convenient spacing for your purposes. The spacing will also vary if you want to slow-in and slow-out.

After marking the pan chart on the artwork, place the background on the baseboard in the start position and put a small arrow or some other reference mark on the baseboard next to the first mark on the chart. After exposing one frame (two if you are double framing), slide the background until the next mark on the pan chart lines up with the arrow on the baseboard — and so on.

The speed of the horizontal movement in your finished film will depend on the distance between the marks on the pan chart. The greater the distance, the faster the movement. Remembering that you will expose 24 frames for each second of projected film, you will have to decide how fast your objects should appear to move and calibrate the

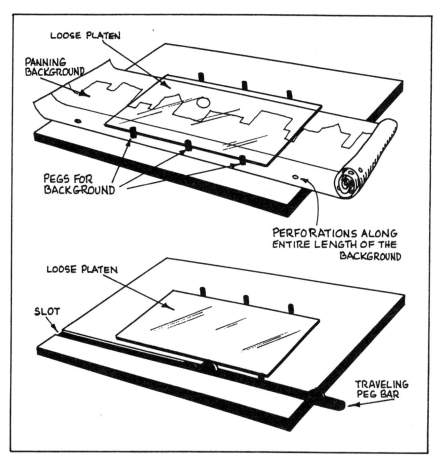

Fig. 83 An extra set of register pegs can be installed for the background or a traveling peg bar can be purchased. Both methods require a new arrangement for the platen. Use of a peg bar means you will need special perforations in the background art.

Fig. 84 A pan chart has been marked along the top edge of this panning background to guide the speed of its (and the hippo's) movements. Note that the animator has marked each movement as it was made in order to keep track of the exposures. If the background is to be used again, mark another pan chart on a strip of paper and glue it over the original one.

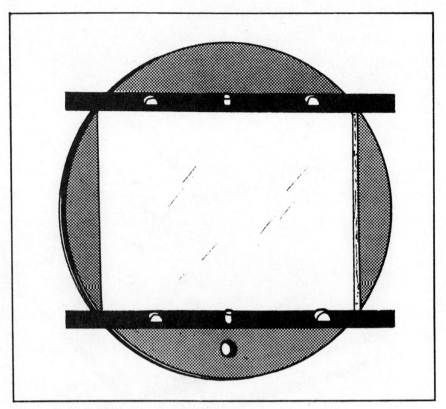

Fig. 85 *An animation disc helps in diagonal and vertical panning.*

fourths or eighths, establishes the spacing of the pan chart on the background.

TICK IT OFF!

You've already learned the importance of checking off each frame on your dope sheet immediately after the frame is exposed. It is just as important to mark the progress of a panning background on the pan chart immediately after each movement is made. If you are interrupted in the shooting routine, even for a moment, can you remember if you really did move the background in preparation for the next exposure? Or didn't you?

A common method of keeping track is to draw a line connecting each successive mark on the pan chart (Figure 84) as the mark is moved past the reference point in the baseboard.

ALL-PURPOSE SCALE

The speed of the background movement varies with the nature of the action it is supporting, so you may find yourself providing each panoramic background with its own special spacing on the pan chart. But if you plan to use a particular background for several sequences, you can give it an all-purpose pan chart scale, even though it will be used

spacing on the pan chart accordingly.

Do not make the spacing too large in order to speed up the movement. This will result in spasmodic jerks of motion. Rather, keep the space between marks as small as is practicable and move the background more often. To get maximum speed, shoot the movement on ones.

TIMING TEAMWORK

The calibration of background movement is especially important when an animated figure appears to be in actual contact with the background. A walking girl, for instance, is in touch with the ground she treads on. Normal walking is about 120 steps per minute, or 2 steps per second. The illusion of the girl's stride is spoiled if the rate of movement of the ground appears to be faster or slower than the motion of her legs. The lateral movement of the background must be coordinated with the

girl's pace in any given segment of time.

This would seem to indicate that, if you are double framing the girl's leg movements, you must also double frame the background movement. This is not always true, however.

As an illustration, let us say you are animating on cels a little man like the one described in the chapter on cutouts. His full stride is 2 inches (5cm), which has been drawn as four leg movements, each covering one-fourth the distance. You can shoot the background movement on twos along with the animation cels, moving it ½ inch (1.25cm) every two exposures, and get a reasonably good result. But the background movement will be much smoother and the entire effect improved, if you change the position of the background after every exposure, moving it only ¼ inch (6.3 mm) each time.

In this case the length of the stride of the animated man, divided into

Fig. 86 *(opposite page) Two backgrounds are used in this sequence involving a hunted hunter. The moon and sky are on Level 1 and the silhouetted forest is on a transparent cel at Level 3. The hunter is on a transparent panning cel between the two levels. The bear's movements are on a cycle of action cels at the top level. Use of a silhouette for the bushes and trees eliminates the need to show the hunter's moving legs. Hence, he can be drawn only once on the panning cel.*

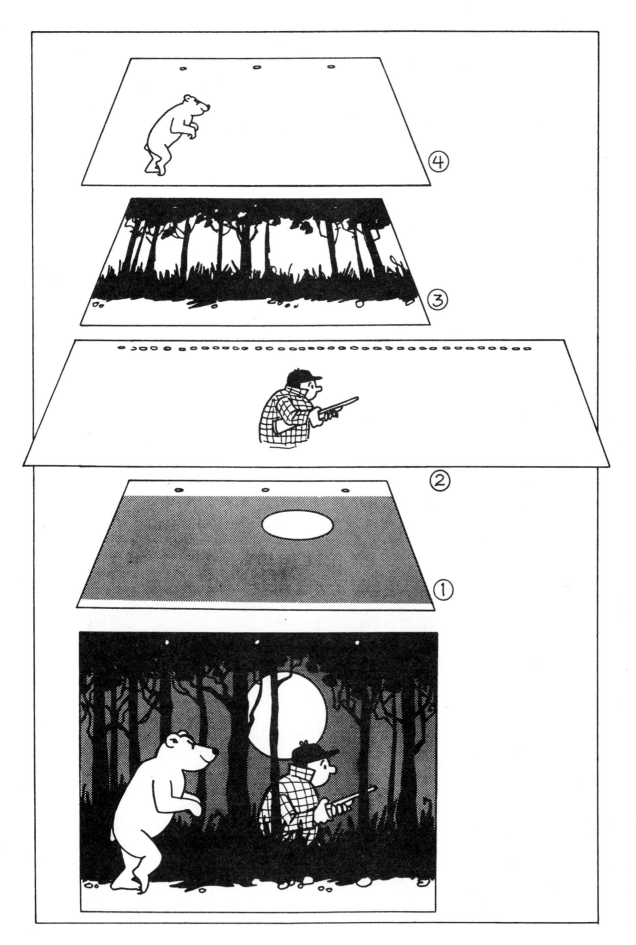

Fig. 87 *The background for this sequence involves two levels and a vertical pan. Level 1: The sun, a single drawing on a blank panoramic sky, pans downward until below the horizon. Level 2: A "scenic" stationary background painted on a transparent cel, including the dock on which the artist sits. Levels 3 and 4: The movements of the artist and his equipment on action cels. Note that once the artist starts to walk off the dock with his catch, the registering arrangement must be switched to accommodate a horizontal pan.*

with actions of different rates of speed. Mark it in increments of $1/8$ inch or perhaps $1/2$ centimeter. For each separate action sequence, mark the appropriate distances of background movement on the scale with erasable pencil marks.

If the action starts and/or stops with your animated figure in view, don't forget to allow for slowing-in and slowing-out. This will mean closer spacing on the pan chart at one or both ends of the movement.

VERTICAL AND DIAGONAL PANNING

While most animation panning is done horizontally (east-west), you may also want to pan in other directions, particularly up and down (north-south) to show objects rising and falling. Since things would get a bit hairy if you tried to install peg bars that go both horizontally and vertically on the same baseboard, prepare a second, detachable baseboard designed and equipped specifically for vertical panning. It may also be able to provide for pans on a diagonal. Examples of diagonal pans would be a figure going up or down a stairway or a skier gliding down a slope. In either case, it is important that registration of the background and animation cels be worked out in advance.

A professional approach to multi-directional panning, and therefore a more costly one, is to get yourself an *animation disc* (Figure 85). To install it in the baseboard of your animation stand, you will have to cut a large circular hole. But the versatility provided by the movable disc may outweigh the trouble and cost.

MULTI-LEVEL BACKGROUNDS

If your storyboard indicates that a

Fig. 88 *A foreground painted on a transparent cel can be used with or without a background. Foregrounds are especially useful in creating an illusion of depth.*

figure must move *behind* a portion of the background (Figure 86), you will have to prepare the background on two levels and *sandwich* the action between them. In the example shown, the moon and sky are on a stationary background, which is the bottom level next to the baseboard. The silhouetted trees are on a separate transparent cel. The hunter moves between the two layers and the bear is on cels atop the sandwich. (Note that the silhouetted brush and grass have been made high enough to avoid having to animate the hunter's leg movements.)

Here's an opportunity to test your ability to plan a multi-level background arrangement. Before you read the descriptive caption under the segment of storyboard showing the fishing artist (Figure 87), see if you can determine the cel levels required and their order in the cel sandwich.

FOREGROUNDS ADD DEPTH

Quite often a foreground is used in conjunction with a background to add depth to a scene. With a proper foreground, you can even dispense with the background and still provide an impression of depth (Figure 88). The foreground can be painted in detail or be shown as a silhouette, depending on the nature of the action, the style of your drawing, or the mood you wish to impart. Foreground silhouettes are often useful in aiding the impression of depth when doing over-the-camera animation.

Foregrounds, like backgrounds, are also panned east and west. If there is simultaneous movement on animation cels beneath a panning foreground, a pan chart like the one discussed earlier for backgrounds is even more important. This is because the foreground artwork must be raised to permit each change in the action cels. It is imperative that you replace the foreground in the correct position each time.

NOW YOU SEE IT, NOW YOU DON'T

Once you've established a background for an action, it isn't necessary for it to hang in there all the time. For instance, you show a man at a desk in an office. He rises and paces back and forth before a blank background (the viewer still imagines the office). You reestablish the office background when the man resumes his seat at the desk.

Some animators use visual shorthand, drawing a single object or part of one to achieve imaginative backgrounds. A case in point is the lady (Figure 89) who goes through a door, the only other object on the screen. Is she going in or out? Is she at home or in a pizza parlor? As the action continues and it becomes apparent what she is doing, the viewer graciously supplies imaginary details for the background. (It so happens the little old lady has entered a newspaper editor's office. She gives him what for with her umbrella.)

Fig. 89 *A single object — in this case, a door — can be used successfully as an entire background for the action.*

In the firing squad scene (Figure 90), from an experimental film titled *Banana Republic*, there was no need to include a background wall or palm trees, because of the costuming and action. Nevertheless, the Latin American setting is there in the mind's eye of the viewer.

TO AND FROM THE CAMERA

You can even provide the illusion of a third dimension in blank backgrounds by the way you treat the animation. One way is with animation in depth, like a rhinoceros lumbering toward the camera (Figure 91). Another way to get the rhino into your lap is with a series of horizontal cycles, each one closer than its predecessor. Beginning at a level about halfway up the frame, show the rhino in very small drawings entering the frame from one side and rushing across to exit on the other. After a second's pause, he re-enters the frame and races across in the opposite direction. This time he is a bit larger and a bit lower in the frame.

Fig. 90 *There is no need to paint a background if the objects, costumes, or action will create the desired locale in the imagination of your audience. This scene is from a film entitled* Banana Republic.

110

Continue this zigzag action in as many cycles as you wish. Be sure that the imaginary baseline for the rhino's feet is lower in each horizontal pass and that the rhino is larger. The level of his back may even rise in the frame to reinforce the illusion that he is getting nearer and larger. A version of this zigzag action is illustrated in Figure 56 on page 75.

RANDOM BACKGROUND NOTES

- To add another dynamic dimension to a panning background, zoom in or out with the camera as you pan. If you zoom out, that is, back away to a long shot, remember that the camera's field size will increase and that you must provide for this larger area on the background.

- Backgrounds for cel animation should be fastened to the baseboard along one edge only. Do not tape down the other sides. If you do, the background will tend to hump in the middle when the glass platen is lifted from it. A background attached or pegged only along one edge will "float" back into a perfectly flat position.

- Since cels should be pressed flat against the background (by the platen) to avoid cast shadows, it may be necessary to put padding beneath your backgrounds. This is especially true if you use parallel cardboard strips as guides for a panning background. Pad underneath with a paper towel or some other sort of crinkly, compressible tissue.

- Textured and varicolored backgrounds (textiles, burlap, lace, crepe paper, sandpaper, window screen, etc.) make exciting substitutes for blank backgrounds. Animated figures photographed over them should be whited-in or

painted with opaque colors.

- Make stationary backgrounds quickly and economically on a large sketch pad, 18" x 24" (45 x 60 cm). Avoid glossy paper.

- Painted backgrounds, even those on stiff illustration board, have a nasty habit of crinkling or undulating. To avoid this, take a tip from watercolorists and pre-stretch the background paper you paint on. Here's how:

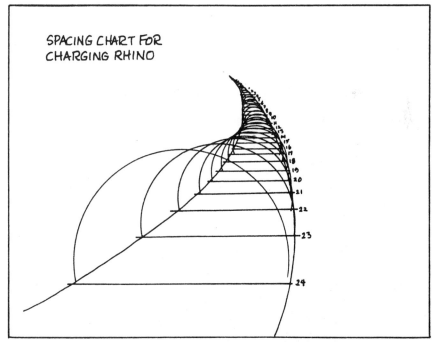

SPACING CHART FOR CHARGING RHINO

Fig. 91 *The approach of this rhinoceros toward the camera requires many action drawings, each larger than its predecessor. A spacing chart of the rhinoceros's size and movements should be worked out before you start drawing. Another way to depict the approach of the rhinoceros is to draw a cycle of two to four drawings to show his leg movements, then shoot the ever-growing figure with the aid of a zoom lens.*

Place a sheet of good quality paper slightly larger than you need on a smooth surface. Tape it down on all four sides, using wide masking tape. Sponge the paper with clean water until it is thoroughly wet. When dry, mark the positions where the register holes will be punched, then paint your background. Cut the background loose from the tape after the paint is thoroughly dry.

BACKGROUNDS FOR THREE-DIMENSIONAL SETS

Puppets and three-dimensional objects can be animated against flat backgrounds—drawings, paintings, enlarged photographs, collages, and textured materials. Mount them on stiff backing, and with some ingenuity you may even be able to devise ways to pan the backgrounds as the action is filmed in front of them.

In most cases, however, highly effective three-dimensional animation is achieved when the flat, pictorial, or textured background serves only as a backdrop for other objects nearer the camera. If it is designed as a stage with flats and props, or as a miniature movie set, your three-dimensional setup can be a versatile arena for a variety of actions and numerous animated sequences. After exposing one sequence, change the position of the camera and get a whole new slant on your story.

As was mentioned in Chapter 9, care must be taken in planning a three-dimensional set to avoid unsightly shadows. It must be large enough and arranged so as to permit free movement of the objects. It must be large enough all around to fill the camera field of vision with each change of shooting angle.

13

SPECIAL EFFECTS

Special effects is a magic term in film making, because it refers to the imaginative tricks and illusions that bring ooohs and aaahs from theater audiences. Needless to say, a few successful special effects can greatly enhance a reel of animated film.

Generally, animation special effects are produced in two ways: with camera techniques and with art techniques. The first are the same camera tricks that are used in live-action films. The art techniques, on the other hand, are what give animation its unique properties. The preparation and manipulation of special artwork achieves the "impossible," making people, animals, and objects cut fantastic capers that you won't see in live-action movies.

So let's look at some basic animation special effects — the ones that are easy to do.

CAMERA TECHNIQUES

Fade-In, Fade-Out

You have seen *fades* hundreds of times in movies and television. At the beginning, the screen is dark and the picture gradually appears (fades in), becoming brighter and brighter. At the end of the film, with the hero and heroine living happily ever after, the picture fades out to a dark screen again. This fading in and out is also used to make transitions from one scene to another.

When filming a fade in animation, you increase the light or decrease the light as you expose each frame. You can double frame or triple frame the changes in light intensity, but a fade will be smoother if you make exposure adjustments after shooting each frame.

One way to do this is to adjust the lens aperture on the camera, perhaps one f stop for each change. Care must be taken to avoid jiggling the camera. Another method is to reduce or increase the light at its source. Attach a dimming device to your floodlamp switch and use it to fade in or out.

Dissolves

A *dissolve* is an optical effect frequently seen in professional films, but beyond the capabilities of most beginners. One scene gradually fades out as another appears, with the impression of a double exposure in the middle. The handling of the light intensity is the tricky part. You must also have a rewind feature on your camera to do an effective dissolve. It is best to pass it over for now and try some of the other equally interesting effects in the animator's bag of tricks.

Focus Pull

Film makers can't seem to decide whether this effect is called a *focus pull* or *pull focus*. But everyone agrees it can add intriguing touches to a film. Yet it is nothing more than getting a scene in or out of focus. For example, you shoot the title or opening scene of your film so that it will be blurred and out of focus. Then, by adjusting the camera's focusing ring, you gradually bring the images into sharp definition.

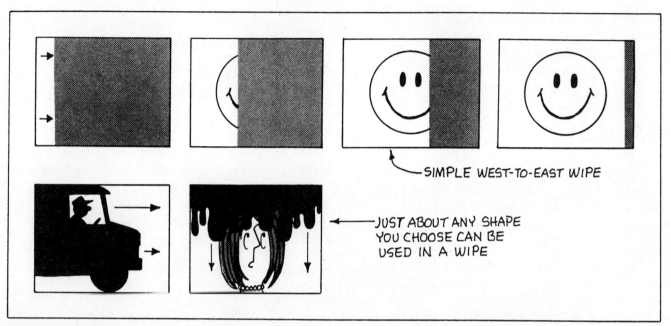

SIMPLE WEST-TO-EAST WIPE

JUST ABOUT ANY SHAPE YOU CHOOSE CAN BE USED IN A WIPE

Fig. 92 *The simplest wipe of all is a vertical line moving across the screen to wipe on or wipe off a picture. One picture can be wiped on as it pushes another off. Wipes don't have to move side-to-side, however, and they can take any shape you please.*

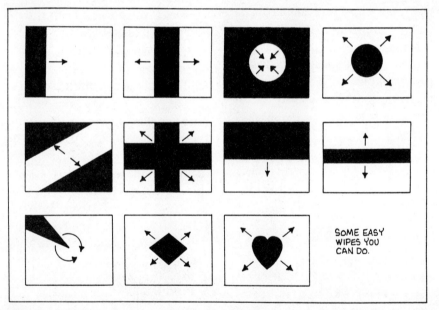

SOME EASY WIPES YOU CAN DO.

Fig. 93 *Some standard wipes used by film makers. There are 120 in the repertoire.*

Another trick of focus pull is used in three-dimensional animation. You start with an object in the foreground in sharp focus and the background blurred. Then adjust the camera lens so the foreground goes out of focus and objects in the background take on clarity.

ART TECHNIQUES

Wipes

A *wipe* is so named because it appears to do just that. It wipes a scene off or onto the screen. Professionals accomplish this as a camera technique, using dark mats, a rewind facility, and so forth. But you can do wipes by manipulating artwork instead. Use them to make scenes emerge from a blank screen or disappear bit by bit. Also use them to get from one scene to another in a much more interesting fashion than with a cut or dissolve.

In its simplest form (Figure 92), a vertical line moves across the screen like an advancing tide across a sandy beach. The scene in its path disappears as the advancing line sweeps across it and a second scene emerges behind the line.

But that's just for openers. Instead of a straight line traveling in one direction, the outlines of wipes can be an unlimited grab-bag of shapes. The shapes can move in any or all directions at one time. They can expand or contract. Some of the possibilities are shown in Figure 93.

Silhouettes

Entire animated films have been made using silhouettes alone, though this is seldom done in modern animation. Nevertheless, silhouettes have valuable uses in cel and cutout animation. They are used in regular animation for a visual change of pace, to establish a mood, to reawaken interest, and, in many cases, to indicate a nighttime action. The silhouetted man snoring at the opera (Figure 95) was used to add an additional touch of humor to the scene.

Swish

This bit of visual hocus-pocus is usually expressed as a cluster of parallel speed lines that substitute for a rapidly moving figure (Figure 96). The illusion is that the body is moving too fast to be seen clearly. What's more, the speed lines make things easier for the animator. Seeing the *swish*, the viewer's imagination readily assumes a change in the position of the grasshopper's legs. There is no need to draw numerous inbetweens of the grasshopper to show the change. To animate a swish, move it or the background *fast*.

Squash

If a swish comes, can a squash be far behind? A *squash* (also shown in Figure 96) is an exaggerated compacting of an object when it strikes the ground or another object. The sudden flattening of the object, or whatever it hits, humorously implies the consequences of speed or force ending in a sudden impact.

A good squash demonstrates, probably best of all art techniques, the ingredient of "impossibility" that makes animated cartoons unique. A small bird flies into a brick wall and causes the wall to squash inward. The improbability of the act makes it funny. A heavy safe falls from a height and flattens a cartoon character, normally a tragic event. But he quickly springs back to his original shape and scampers off — and the audience roars with laughter.

Stretch and Drag

Another way to tamper with physical laws is the animated *stretch*, a

---

HOW TO WIPE

To do a simple wipe of one scene to reveal another:

1. Fasten one drawing (the scene to be wiped off) to a pane of glass, using a few small dabs of rubber cement.
2. Register a drawing of the second scene on the baseboard pegs.
3. Position the drawing attached to the glass directly over the one on the baseboard.
4. Expose two frames of the top drawing; then cut a narrow strip off one side. Lateral wipes commonly go from left to right, so start cutting on the left side.
5. Continue slicing strips from the top drawing, exposing two or three frames each time. The top drawing will appear to wipe away, revealing the scene beneath it.

Study this simple cutting-away method and consider how it can be applied to make wipes shaped like an expanding circle, a diamond, a star, a spiraling ribbon, and more.

A variation of the *cutaway wipe* is a *push-off wipe*. In the push-off method, you don't use the pane of glass. Instead, you cut the top drawing into parts (Figure 94) and reassemble the picture directly on top of the scene on the register pegs. Gradually move the separate parts outward, exposing two frames after each shift of position.

Fig. 94 *An example of a push-off wipe. A picture is cut into parts and reassembled on the baseboard on top of a second picture. The cut parts are then moved outward and out of the field of vision to reveal a second picture.*

Fig. 95 *The silhouetted foreground in this scene not only establishes an audience for the singer, it adds to the action. The Z's were animated, rising from the head of the snoring man.*

deliberate lengthening of a figure beyond credibility, due to opposing physical forces — movement vs. inertia, for example. A trash man (Figure 97) tries to lift a heavy can from the ground. It stretches out of shape, but its base remains unmoved. A snail leaps forward. For a moment the front portion of its body is elongated until the rear end gets a move on and catches up with the rest.

A *drag* is a form of stretch. It is the exaggerated distortion of an object in motion or when it starts and stops. In the drawings of a truck (Figure 97), the supposedly rigid truck body bends backward or forward, according to how the animator tampers with inertia.

Assorted Energizers

Making things "come alive" is the whole purpose of animation. If you have things in your film that normally vibrate, wiggle, and waver, you don't want them just to sit there. Make the stars in the night sky twinkle, candles flicker, alarm clocks jangle, hearts beat, and more. It takes as little as two drawings to carry out each type of movement.

As an example, you can animate a drawing of a campfire (Figure 98) by drawing a duplicate picture with the flames slightly larger or smaller. After shooting the first fire on twos, substitute the second cel and make two exposures of it. Repeat this back-and-forth substitution. The result will be the illusion of flickering flames. To heighten the illusion further, draw the tips of the flames on the second cel to the left and right of the flame tips in the first drawing.

A pulsing heart, a throbbing sore thumb, or twinkling stars are more examples of "live" objects that can be animated in this two-cel manner. In the second drawing of a sky full of stars, make some of the stars larger and some smaller than the originals. A similar treatment was used in the case of the man with spots before his eyes (Figure 99).

To show an object about to burst (Figure 100), use the two-cel cycle and also borrow a visual trick from the comic strips. Draw "vibration lines" around the objects and make these lines pulsate just as the objects do.

Remember also that changing colors in the cel cycles will increase the illusion of vibrant life, especially in things like flames, which alternate between red and yellow. Take a hint from our colorful language and make your animated characters turn blue with cold, red with anger, and green with envy.

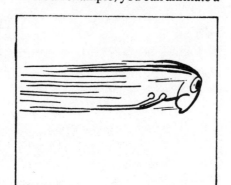

Fig. 96 *A hapless hopper demonstrates a swish (center) and a squash.*

Smoke, Clouds, and Wispy Things

To show moving clouds and smoke, break one of animation's rules and white them in with soft edges on *top* of the cels. Paint a cycle of cels being not too careful about getting the sizes or edges the same, and your clouds and smoke will act more like real clouds and smoke.

Another way to achieve this effect is to paint a cloud or clouds on the top of a cel and retouch the edges at intervals during the shooting. You might even experiment with water-base paints that can be scrubbed away bit by bit to make the clouds disperse. Both these add-on and scrub-off tricks can be especially helpful in improving a panning background of clouds or smoke.

Transparent effects such as smoke, mists, ghosts, and odors from mom's apple pie can be put on cels with semi-transparent paint so that your animated characters and backgrounds will show through them. It is difficult to get a consistent transparent tone from cel to cel, but wispy things are supposed to be mercurial, aren't they?

If your background is dark enough, you can show a transparent bubble or ghostly apparition in white lines on overlying cels. Or you can paint it as white outlines and shoot a sequence against a flat black background. Then wind back the film and

Fig. 98 Two cels, with slight variations on the shape of the same object, can be used alternately to make the object "come alive." The dotted lines in the drawing show how the flames could be drawn on a second cel to make the fire flicker. Try this same principle to animate a waving banner or a girl's hair blowing in the wind.

EXAMPLES OF 'STRETCH' AND 'DRAG'

Fig. 97 In these examples, the trash can and snail demonstrate stretch; the truck shows two ways to use drag. In the drawing of the truck skidding to a stop, the tires are also stretched.

shoot your planned animation with the "ghost" making a guest appearance in the double exposures.

For cutout animation, try using gauze, fine netting, tracing paper, and other semi-transparent materials.

Fig. 99 To show the spots "swimming" before the man's eyes in this segment, the animator dotted them on a series of cels, changing their sizes and position on each cel. Once the psychiatrist got it all together, the big dot at right remained fairly steady.

Fig. 100 A two-cel cycle of the frog's chest and the boy's bubble gum, plus "vibration lines," can be used to animate these two figures.

14

TITLING

You would think a book incomplete if it didn't have a cover bearing the name of the story and its author. That's also true of film titles and credits. The public is so accustomed to seeing lead and end titles on films, plus long lists of the cast and other credits, that a movie without them would seem incomplete — a book without covers.

For this reason alone, you should pay particular attention to preparing titles for your own animated films.

Audiences got hooked on the titling habit back in the days of silent films, when more than just the name and credits was needed to explain the story action. Subtitles such as "Chinatown After Dark" or "Meanwhile Back at the Ranch" made a visual-verbal link that set the scene for the viewer. These "written" aids within the body of a film are not often seen in modern feature films, including animation. But the titling at the beginning and end of films, along with the showing of credits, has become an imaginative art in itself.

Rather than merely flashing on a series of cards giving the film title, author, producers, etc., modern film titlers use all the tricks of the trade — and animation looms large among them. An especially memorable example is the titling for a series of *Pink Panther* motion pictures starring the late Peter Sellers. The name of the movie and all the credits appeared on the screen in an animated sequence featuring a cartoon pan-

ther (pink, of course) and a little trench-coated sleuth. Their antics, plus the novel ways in which the cast's names and credits appeared on the screen, introduced the comic mood of the film that followed. If animation can be outstanding in the titling of a live-action motion picture, it follows that animation titles can do equally well in introducing animation film.

The steady improvements and innovativeness of lead and end titles have not meant that the subtitles of yore are as outmoded as silent films. Subtitles introducing scenes and topics are still used extensively to enhance documentary, training, and sales films. You may find them useful, too, depending on the subjects of your animation, providing the subtitling will help you emphasize, clarify, or otherwise communicate things that the animated action alone can't do.

GENERAL RULES FOR TITLING

As you have surmised by now, a film title (or subtitle) is more than a printed label that just sits there. It can consist of two or more elements: words, graphics, color, motion, and sound. A really good title should:

- Create an ambient mood for the story and characters

- Symbolize and foreshadow that which is to come

- Be clear, both visually and verbally

- Be brief

That's not as tall an order as it looks. Just keep the rules in mind as you create your titles in step-by-step fashion.

Writing

It is best to have a name for your animated film by the time you are ready to produce the titling. Whether you do or don't, this is a very good time to write down all the titles you can think of, plus everything else you want to show in your title and credit sequences.

Study very carefully what you have written — not just for spelling and punctuation but for clarity and to see if you can reduce the number of words. Chances are you can.

Above all, strive for brevity; it's the soul of good titles. Example: The animated film *The Physics Lesson* (see Figure 55 on page 74) was originally titled *A Lesson in Physical Laws* until the author started designing the title sequence. The shorter title not only looked better graphically, it established a greater air of anticipation on the part of the viewer.

Good rules can be broken for the sake of a good cause. While brevity is desirable, it must be weighed against a longer title that more effectively expresses the mood and foretells the nature of the film. The animation storyboard about the little page's troubles with his boss, the drunken knight, could easily have been titled "The Page" or "The Knight" to keep it short. But in the interest of establishing the humorous theme of the film, a punning paraphrase of a much longer statement was chosen as more suitable: *Mother Told Me There Would Be Knights Like This* (Figure 107).

The *Mother Told Me* ... title demonstrates still another element you should strive for when planning your lead titles. Try to arouse the imagi-

Fig. 101 *An example of lettering used to enhance the nature of the filmed subject.*

nation of your audience. When they read your titles, make them want to see what's going to happen.

One more thing: Be understandable. Sometimes in our writing and drawing we know what we want to express, but we assume too much knowledge on the part of the viewer. A title may be crystal clear to us. But it's quite a letdown to have someone say "I don't get it." It's doubly disheartening if they say that after you've gone to the trouble and expense of projecting it. So pre-test your titles and a few alternates by showing them to several friends. Their reactions will help you select the most effective ones. Someone might even spot a misplaced comma!

LETTERING

After you've written and edited the wording of your title, select the typeface or faces you wish to use. Keep in mind that the style and weight of the lettering will have bearing on the "personality" of your title and, by extension, of your entire film.

No matter how you plan to print your titles — by hand-lettering, pressure-sensitive lettering, or other methods — it is a good idea to study a book of type specimens to discover their many characteristics and personalities. Some types are bold and masculine; others are dainty. Some types are lighthearted; others somber. There are fat ones, skinny ones, ornate ones, and workaday ones. You can also find type styles that suggest particular countries or regions of the world (Figure 101). As you become more familiar with typefaces, the innovative quality of your film titles will improve accordingly.

SOURCES OF LETTERING

Professional animators have various sophisticated methods of producing lettering for their titles. But they also use simpler and less expensive methods that are practical for the amateur animator. They are the ones we'll deal with here.

Hand-Lettering — Hand-lettered titles are highly effective when they are well done. (Crude ones can spoil the effect of good animation.) Hand-lettering also provides the animator with two benefits: (1) it costs nothing if you do it yourself, and (2) it gives you carte blanche — a wide range of creative opportunities for printing and writing exciting film titles. Some of the techniques will be discussed later on.

Dry-Transfer Lettering — Variously called pressure-sensitive type, press-type, and other names, dry-transfer lettering is probably the most practical for the amateur animator, next to hand-lettering. Dry-transfer letters are on very thin translucent sheets. The individual letters will stick to almost any surface when they are rubbed or "burnished" on. This makes dry-transfer type an ideal source of neat, professional-looking lettering for use on animation artwork, including the acetate sheets used in cel animation.

You can get sheets of dry-transfer type at almost any art supply store. They are available in an unusually large selection of type styles and sizes, including several colors as well as white type for use on dark or colored backgrounds. Just a few examples of the many dry-transfer lettering styles are shown in Figure 102.

Some dry-transfer trade names most often encountered in art supply stores are Letraset, Chartpak, Zipatone, Formatt, and Mecanorma. Each company supplies a catalog of type styles, borders, and dry-transfer graphic aids. Any of these catalogs is worthy of study to acquaint yourself with the characteristics of type faces. They also give detailed directions for applying the letters.

Three-Dimensional Lettering —If you're doing three-dimensional animation, also consider using three-dimensional letters for your titling to support the major characteristic of your film. These "raised" letters are usually found at art supply houses in the form of white, ceramic block letters in a limited number of styles and sizes. Some wooden ones may also be available. The block letters are relatively inexpensive because they can be used again and again.

Though cast shadows are usually considered thorns in the sides of good animators, the deliberately contrived shadows of three-dimensional letters can add appreciably to the attractiveness of a film title. Do some experimenting with your lighting when you photograph them.

You needn't limit yourself to purchased three-dimensional lettering. With a modicum of skill you can carve your own in wood. On a smaller scale, an assortment of anagram squares or Scrabble® cubes can be used (Figure 103).

Mechanical Lettering — Don't overlook the potentials in using a mechanical lettering set like the ones

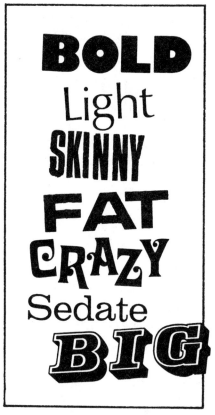

Fig. 102 There are literally hundreds of useful and decorative type styles to choose from in catalogs of dry-transfer lettering.

Fig. 103 These anagram squares were handmade by pressing dry transfer lettering onto illustration board and cutting the letters apart.

121

Fig. 104 *Sandpaper makes a dandy sandy beach for titling. The starfish were a bonus found in a bag of fresh shrimp purchased dockside. The words were painted on to take full advantage of the grainy surface.*

used by draftsmen and map makers. These sets provide a series of alphabets cut as grooves in templates shaped like rulers. A scribing tool containing ink is used to trace the letter patterns onto the title artwork. The type styles are necessarily plain because of the mechanical limitations. But they make up for this with a clarity and neatness that has a charm of its own. Mechanical lettering can be achieved easily and quickly in very small sizes, making it ideal for listing credits and inserting neatly lettered words on charts, diagrams, and other filmed artwork.

A drafting teacher in a local high school or community college can show you how to use a mechanical lettering set. Perhaps he or she can arrange the temporary loan of one.

One of the simplest mechanical lettering templates is a thin plastic one from which the forms of the letters have been cut out, somewhat similar to the forms in a common stencil. This suggests you might also investigate using ordinary stencils when lettering your film titles — provided "blocky" letters are suitable.

DESIGN

The principles of good design that apply to such art as master paintings, magazine layouts, advertisements, and posters apply equally to the layout of good film titles. However, there are no hard and fast rules for you to follow, because the application of design principles will depend on the subject matter and visual styles of your particular animated films. Here are some suggestions for use as general guidelines:

Simplicity — Just as we have seen the virtue of brevity in title wording, simplicity of layout will also enhance your title's visual impact on your audience. Too many type styles or too many type sizes will lessen the clarity of the message. A background that is too busy will weaken the effectiveness of the lettering. Overly ornate design elements and graphic symbols will distract the viewer, as will garish colors and poor color combinations.

Thus, the same rule of thumb applies in designing your titles that you should practice when writing them:

brevity. After sketching a rough layout of everything you want to include in a title — words, graphics, background, colors — see how much you can eliminate or subdue while still maintaining a strong visual-verbal message. You may be surprised how the simpler designs will express more, and more quickly, than the originals.

Emphasis — Something or things should be dominant in every title design. There is bound to be a word or words you wish to stress, or a graphic symbol that rates special attention. In order to make such words or symbols stand out in the design, make them unique. Here are some ways to do it:

- Print key words in larger type than the rest.
- Print key words in a different type face than the rest.
- Print key words in a different color than the rest.
- Underline the key word or words.
- Contrast key words or symbols with the background (dark on light, light on dark).
- Animate key words and symbols.
- Use animation devices to direct attention to key words and symbols (wipes, pans, spotlights, pointing arrows, etc.).

Composition — It is axiomatic to say that composition is an important element of good design. It is, in fact, the most important element. If your title has pictorial or graphic design elements in it, make sure that the basic lines of the composition converge upon or otherwise lead the eye to the important words or symbols of the title.

Backgrounds — Even if you opt for a simple, hand-lettered title, consider increasing its attractiveness, and its symbolic effectiveness, by using a colored and/or textured background for the lettering. Both the color and the texture can help convey the mood and theme of your film. You can use wood grain, for example, to express an outdoor theme, or gingham for a kitchen-centered theme.

A wide variety of textured background materials is ready at hand in and around your home. Just waiting for creative use are wooden panels, burlap, gauze, wallpaper, woven placemats, split bamboo shades, window screening, sandpaper (Figure 104), brick walls, carpet remnants, and more. You can letter directly on many of them, then focus and expose the required number of frames with your movie camera. Fasten thin materials like burlap and sandpaper to the baseboard of your animation stand, just as you would with any artwork background, and place stable or animated cels over them. Take still photographs of thicker or immobile materials and use enlarged prints on your animation stand.

Art supply stores carry large sheets of illustration board in a wide range of colors. Many also have cards with interesting textures. Avoid anything with a glossy or reflective surface. And, of course, be sure you don't select colors or textures that will upstage the lettering of your titles.

COLOR

The correct use of color is immensely important in titling. Color (1) helps establish a mood for your film; (2) symbolizes a theme; (3) helps to emphasize or subdue particular components of the title; and, of course, (4) simply makes the whole thing look a lot better.

In all cases, the colors you use should meet two criteria: *continuity* and *legibility*.

Continuity — When you plan an animated film in color, the nature of your story, its mood or theme, will to a large extent indicate a color scheme that will best convey those features. Continuity, as applied in titles, simply means that the colors in the lead title should introduce the color scheme that will predominate throughout the animation. The subtitles and end title should complement and reinforce this selection.

Just what colors should you select? Alas, the proper use of color, both as a mode of expression and in relation to other colors, is a study in itself. Short of embarking on *that* excursion, we can in the meantime take note of some of the meanings that most of us derive from colors. They are the psychological associations that we have been taught by the traditions of our culture and environment.

Color Symbols — Red and green are for Christmas, black and orange for Halloween, lavender for Easter, green for St. Patrick's Day, shades of brown for Thanksgiving, pink and pale blue for blessed events, pale green for spring, yellow for summer, tans and orange for autumn, white and blue for winter.

EASIEST-TO-READ COLOR COMBINATIONS

1. BLACK ON YELLOW
2. BLACK ON WHITE
3. YELLOW ON BLACK
4. WHITE ON BLACK
5. DARK BLUE ON WHITE
6. WHITE ON DARK BLUE
7. WHITE ON GREEN
8. GREEN ON WHITE
9. RED ON WHITE
10. WHITE ON RED
11. BLACK ON ORANGE
12. ORANGE ON BLACK

Fig. 105 *The lower the number on this list, the higher the visibility.*

Fig. 106 *The black-and-white drawing shown here had to be cut out and placed on a light gray background to minimize glare for a television commercial. You may encounter this problem in your animation if too large an area of your background is white.*

Color Moods and Associations — Yellow is warmth, gaiety, brightness, and optimism. Red is heat, fury, excitement, revolution. Blue is coolness, sadness, serenity. Green is fertility, finance, envy. Purple is royalty, elegance. Black is mourning, solidity. White is purity, and brushing your teeth after meals.

Legibility — Along with continuity you must assure the legibility of the colors in your titles. Some color combinations are highly visible, but others make it hard to discern the words and pictures.

Obviously, the color of title lettering should not be too similar to that in the background. White lettering on yellow would flunk most tests of legibility. On the other hand, black letters on yellow are so easily visible that this combination is the accepted standard for traffic signs. (Some color experts argue that dark blue on yellow is better, but it doesn't make that much difference at 55 miles per hour.)

Many research studies have been conducted to rate the degrees of readability of different color combinations. The resulting lists don't agree in every detail because of different values and intensities of the tested colors. But a generally accepted rating of the twelve most readable color combinations is shown in Figure 105.

You certainly shouldn't limit yourself to the color combinations in the rating list (the colors were tested for viewing outdoors at a distance). But they will serve when you want assured visual impact with legibility. Here are some additional general observations to remember when preparing colored titles. They are based on the experience of professional animators:

- Colored lettering shows up best on a contrasting plain color.

- Cool colors are more visible in lettering than warm colors; rich, dark tones show up best.

- Most reds and various shades of brown project well.

- Pastel shades in backgrounds tend to appear dull and muddy on the screen.

- On the other hand, pastel pencil and pastel stick lettering on black backgrounds usually are very legible.

BLACK AND WHITE

In many cases a textured background can be used to make a black-and-white film title more interesting. But be aware of a problem in contrast that may crop up, because contrast is a greater factor in black-and-white film art than it is when color is used. The textured background will appear as a gray tone. It must be light enough to let the title lettering and graphics show up well. Or, if your background is a dark gray, you should prepare your title lettering in white.

At the same time, avoid overly large white areas in your title frames. If there is too much contrast, the white background will impinge on the black lines and weaken them. (For the same reason, a quick cut from a very light frame to a dark one will result in a temporary loss of clarity in the dark frame. Persistence of vision, remember?)

Figure 106 shows sample frames from a black-and-white television commercial that suffered this problem of contrast. The cartoon characters were borrowed from art prepared on white paper for a companion series of newspaper ads and were animated in stop-motion. A test filming revealed that the black-on-white contrast was too great. The cartoons did not appear sharp and black. All the cartoons were then cut out and pasted on pale gray cards (commonly used by television studios). The subsequent film had greater visual impact.

Should you have doubts about the blackness of the black lines in your titles, or in *any* animation sequence drawn on white animation paper, here's a trick you can use with an exposure meter. With everything ready for shooting on the animation stand, and with lights on, lay a pale gray card over the white animation paper and take a reading on that. The

MOTHER TOLD ME
THERE WOULD BE
KNIGHTS LIKE THIS!

indicated setting will prevent over-exposure of the black lines of your art. In cases where you have white lettering or lines on a black background, take your light reading on a white card laid over the artwork. This will give you the minimum exposure for white. The black will turn out to be solid black. Beautiful!

When shooting titles on textured or photo backgrounds, take a reading for each setup, just in case.

Incidentally, "rules" like those above are like political campaign promises. They seem to solve your problems, but they must be bent and tampered with to suit individual conditions.

TITLE PRODUCTION TECHNIQUES

A great deal of what you learned in the chapter on special effects is particularly helpful in titling. Adapt the various tricks of the trade as well as standard animation techniques to introduce your films with a flair.

Here is a distillation of techniques applied specifically to titles.

Stationary Titles

There is no reason a well-designed title can't be attractive, funny, or exciting enough to stand on its own for an entry into your animated film. But also consider the exciting possibilities in the extra touches that follow. The first group includes the things you can do with two-dimensional titles. The camera does the work while the title just lies there looking good.

Zooms — Zooming in or out is generally more successful with simple title wording and design. You can:

- Start with the title at infinity and zoom in on it until the lettering is the full, readable size you want. Hold the full title for two or three seconds.

- Zoom in as above, but continue the zoom until the key word of the title dominates the frame (Figure 107). You can zoom in on a graphic design or symbol instead, especially if it's a visual expression of what the film is all about.

- Open with the title lettering at readable size, hold in there for two or three seconds, then zoom out from it until the title seems to disappear in the distance. This gives you a blank screen from which you can cut or fade to the credits or the opening frame of the animation.

Focus Pull — Use the focusing ring on your camera lens to achieve this. Start with the title blurred and out of focus and gradually bring it into sharp definition. Or reverse the procedure, blurring the title in preparation for a transition to the next sequence.

Focus pull works especially well in three-dimensional animation titles. Hand letter or adhere dry-transfer lettering to a flat background for your scene, then pull the title words in or out of focus. An impressive opening for your film would be to start with the title clear and readable on the background. Next, adjust the lens gradually until the title is blurred and the objects in the foreground come into sharp focus. This provides the "curtain opening" scene of the action that is to follow.

Fig. 107 An extra long title (usually avoided in animation) becomes exciting by: (1) using a figure of the knight as the first letter of the word "knight"; (2) zooming in to a close-up of the key word; (3) animating the knight so he walks away from the title and begins the action of the film.

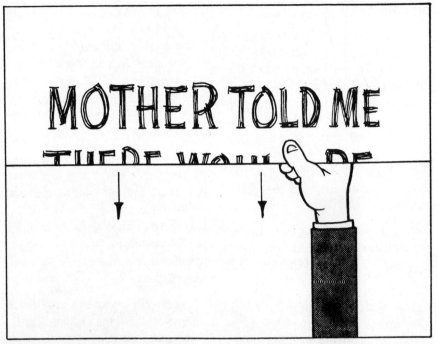

Fig. 108 *Added interest has been given this north-south wipe by having a hand pull the horizontal line down to wipe on a title.*

Fig. 109 *To film this pop-on title, the animator painted the crossword squares on paper and fastened it to the baseboard. The letters of the title were drawn in one at a time following exposures on twos.*

Fades — Fading in on a title is a lot more interesting than abruptly opening on it — BANG — there it is — take it or leave it! The fade-in creates a measure of anticipation and arouses audience interest as the title emerges from a darkened screen. The fade-out is a natural transition to credits or the opening action. Fade-in and fade-out were discussed at the beginning of Chapter 12.

Wipes — Creative wipes are sure-fire attention-getters. For example, a push-off wipe (see Figure 94 on page 115) provides an interesting transition from one title to the next or to the opening scene. By using a north-south wipe (Figure 108) you can introduce a title line by line on a blank screen or wipe it off for the next scene.

Animated Titles

In the preceding techniques, the "action" was achieved by manipulating the camera lens or something other than the title artwork. Now let's look at ways of getting the art itself into the act.

Pop-On — This is one of the easiest methods of animating titles. Pop-ons are seen often on television and movie screens. One letter of a word appears at a time, or entire words pop on until the message is complete. You can pop your whole title, or parts of it, on and off to get a now-you-see-it-now-you-don't effect.

Work directly on the animation stand, lettering on illustration board or designed background. Or use three-dimensional letters, anagram squares, or letters and words cut from publications. Expose three or four frames of the first letter or word, add the second and shoot more frames, and so on (Figure 109).

Pop on pictorial elements, too. Or you can cut your title artwork into jigsaw puzzle pieces and reassemble them on the screen by popping on a piece at a time.

The timing of the pop-on titles depends on the tempo of your film. But a standard and safe timing for popping on letters to spell a word is to hold each letter for six frames before adding the succeeding letter. After the entire title is spelled out, hold it for 72 frames (3 seconds).

Fig. 110 *Cutout letters can be made to move about on the baseboard until they assemble themselves into a title.*

Stop-Motion — This is such a fast-paced, exciting technique a whole chapter is devoted to it (Chapter 6). Stop-motion is especially good for titles with pictorial elements — symbols, drawings of your animated characters, clips from photographs or old steel engravings, etc. As in the pop-on method, stop-motion can be used to introduce the principal characters of your film before the story action begins.

Add-Ons — This technique, which makes a word or picture grow before the eyes of the viewer, is described in Chapter 11 (see Figure 72 on page 95). Use it when there is script lettering in your title. Start with a blank frame or the first letter of a word and add short segments of the succeeding letters between four-frame or six-frame exposures. The title will appear to write itself.

Metamorphosis — A three-dimensional version of the add-on method is to transform an ordinary object into a word or another object. This metamorphosis is accomplished by reshaping the object bit by bit between groups of exposures. It takes a pliable or limber object, of course

— a cord, a length of rope, a dog leash, a very limber wire.

If forming letters proves too difficult, remember that you can use metamorphosis to animate design elements of your titles. For example, in the title of a film with a nautical theme, a coil of rope can unwind and form a frame around the words in the title.

Another version of this technique (Figure 110) is to cause a jumble of animated letters to mill about until they regroup themselves into words. Carried a step further, the words can then break apart and the letters regroup to form still another name or message. Anagram squares are ideal for this sort of jumbled word game. Or put dry-transfer letters on clear acetate and cut them apart (Figure 103).

Pans — Reread the description of panning backgrounds in Chapter 12, and you have another method of animating titles. The title is moved into the frame from one side, usually west to east. You can continue the movement off the other side of the frame, leaving a blank screen for the next sequence.

Working with flat artwork, you'll need a traveling peg bar or the improvised cardboard guide strips described in Chapter 12. But this means you can also use additional cel layers and animate all or part of the title as it pans.

For an interesting title pan for use with a three-dimensional animated film, paint your title on a fence, wall, or other textured background and pan the camera along the lettering. This puts you in the standard motion picture business, but it's very compatible with animation.

CREATIVE COMBINATIONS

Let yourself go. You don't have to stick with just one of the titling techniques at a time. Combine them, blend them to your advantage. A combination of panning and straight animation has just been mentioned. Another natural combination is zoom and pop-on. Zoom in on a graphic symbol or a drawing of one of the characters in your film, then pop on the name of the film all at once or word by word. It's your choice; you're in the creative catbird seat.

15

ADDING SOUND

We are so accustomed to hearing sound with the pictures we see on movie and television screens, even if it is only the background music, that it is hard to imagine producing an animated film without sound — "professional" quality film, that is.

At the beginning, however, you may find it best to limit yourself to silent films until you have mastered the basics of animation itself. This is logical — even recommended. But the time inevitably arrives when you'll want to graduate to the complete package, adding the extra dimension of sound to your films. There are several choices available.

TYPES OF SOUND FOR ANIMATION

The sound, or audio, portion of a film is generally classified into these five categories:

- **Background Music**, which simply complements the visuals, reinforcing the mood and tempo of the action.

- **Background Noises**, which give credibility to the scene (traffic noises, roar of a crowd, crickets chirping, students snoring in study hall).

- **Special Sound Effects**, which are created to reinforce the visual effects (bang of gun, clop of horse's hooves, thud of a falling person or object).

- **Voice-Over**, a narration by a speaker not seen on the screen.

- **Dialogue**, the sound of conversation or speeches by on-screen characters.

You can use one or any combination of the five. Most good animated films include at least four — background music and noises, special sound effects, and dialogue—though many award-winning films don't have the latter. Voice-over, with or without the other types of sound, is used most often in documentary and training films.

Don't let the list trouble you. Some outstanding animated films have been produced with nothing more than a few sound effects at strategic points. It really depends on the nature of the animation and whether it will be effective with or without certain types of sound.

The short film, *The Physics Lesson* (Figure 55 on page 74), is an example of this. It was produced with music and special sound effects only. The animator could also have provided synchronized voice sounds (dialogue) for the four brief statements in the film. But in the interest of simplicity, and since this was a learning exercise similar to what you may be doing, the dialogue was accomplished by popping on visual speech balloons.

As a matter of fact, the use of speech balloons doesn't rule out using dialogue on the sound track at the same time. Research has established that a combination of visible and audible words is more effective as a memory aid than one or the other used alone. You will remember a word on the screen longer if you hear it at the same time you see it. That is why the sound track in the best television commercial speaks the sponsor's sales pitch or slogan at the same time and exactly as the printed words appear on the screen.

THE CHICKEN OR THE EGG?

The question that confronts the inex-

perienced animator is which comes first, the animation or the sound?

Action First, Sound Later

It is possible to make all the drawings and photograph an animated

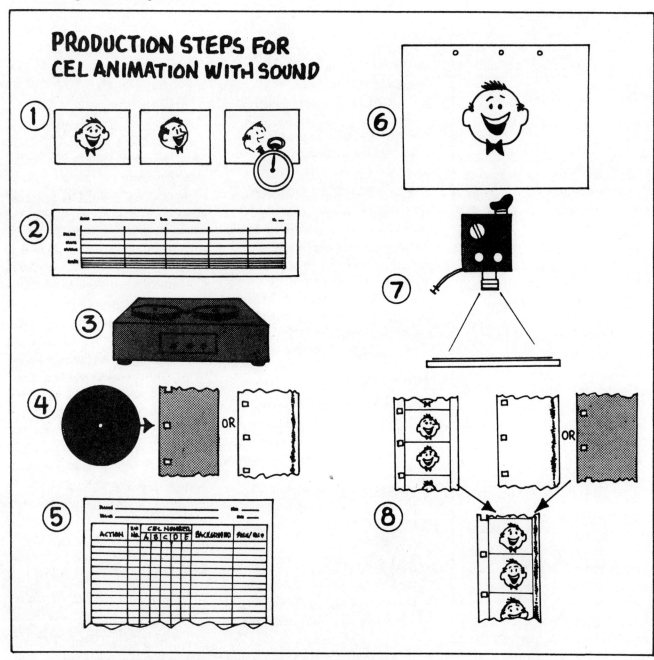

Fig. 111 *Here is the least expensive procedure for assembling a first class sound-first animated film: (1) write and draw a storyboard and carefully time the sounds, dialogue, and music with a stopwatch; (2) transfer the timing information to a bar sheet; (3) record the sound effects, music, and dialogue on 1/4-inch tape; (4) have a processing lab transfer the taped sound to a sound track on magnetic or optical film (as a beginner, you will do better with magnetic film); (5) play the sound track — carefully checking the sound against the storyboard action — and plot the combination of sounds and actions on a dope sheet that has camera shooting instructions; (6) paint the background and cels, using the directions from the dope sheet as your guide; (7) shoot the artwork, using the dope sheet as your guide; (8) send the completed film and sound track film to the lab to be combined in a married print.*

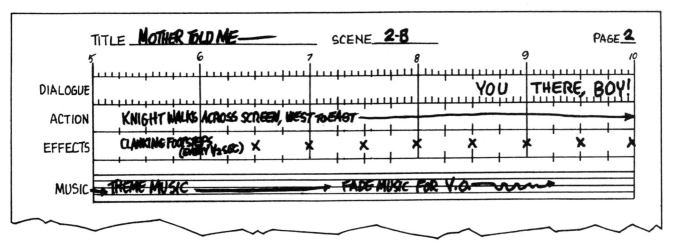

TITLE _MOTHER TOLD ME_ — SCENE _2-B_ PAGE _2_

DIALOGUE: YOU THERE, BOY!

ACTION: KNIGHT WALKS ACROSS SCREEN, WEST TO EAST —

EFFECTS: CLANKING FOOTSTEPS (EVERY ½ SEC) X X X X X X X X

MUSIC: THEME MUSIC → FADE MUSIC FOR V.O. —

Fig. 112 A section of a bar sheet. The numbers are for 1-second increments (V.O. on the bottom line means Voice-over).

film, then add a sound track. Professionals don't recommend this, but even they sometimes do it when they are using background music only, or simply a voice-over, on the sound track.

You can do this, too, assuming you know in advance what the music or the narration is to be. At the point (discussed in an earlier chapter) when you begin timing the actions indicated on your storyboard and putting the details of frame exposures on the dope sheet, you should coordinate the tempo of this information with the tempo of your anticipated music or the oral pace of your voice-over script.

Using a stopwatch, time the music for beat and accents. Say aloud the words of your voice-over narration at the desired rate of speed, making notes of the timing of paragraph endings or other key points and pauses. Translate this information in terms of frames-per-second when you plan the dope sheet. If all goes as planned, when the animation is drawn and filmed, and the sound is eventually recorded, you'll have nicely synchronized audio and video components to marry — and they'll live happily in your sound film.

Sound First, Action Later

The question comes up here, if you're going to all that trouble of rehearsing and timing the sound, why not record it and be done with it? Why not, indeed. Experienced animators will tell you that it is a great deal more *accurate* to record the sound first and match the action to it. Even Walt Disney, the creator of the first animation with sound, learned this lesson at an early stage. As a result, the act of precisely matching action to the beat of pre-recorded music is now called *Mickey Mousing*.

A pre-recorded sound track is a practical necessity if you intend to have audible dialogue with your film. This permits you to make drawings and expose frames so that the lip movements of the characters on the screen are closely synchronized with the oral syllables the audience hears. This is called *lip-sync*.

Animation studios record sound directly on magnetic film, because they are equipped to carry out the whole operation of recording, filming, combining, and processing. In your own case, without elaborate equipment, you can:

- Record your sound on quarter-inch magnetic tape, using an ordinary tape recorder.

- Shoot your animation on film with a magnetic sound track, matching

the action to the sounds on the separate tape.

- Have a commercial film processor equipped to handle sound films "marry" the film and tape and return a completed sound film. That cost is not exorbitant, nor is it much more than the cost of processing a silent film.

A more sophisticated and professional version of this is to record dialogue, music, and sound effects on separate tapes to assure the fidelity of each type of sound, and bring them all together into a master sound track married to the animation in the processing laboratory. But, as we pointed our earlier, such highly technical and expensive methods are beyond the scope and intent of this book.

SOUND-FIRST PROCEDURE

So let's say you're going to create an animated film with synchronized sound. Here's the way to do it (Figure 111):

Step 1 — The Storyboard

Start as you would for any film and rough out your story on a storyboard. Using a stopwatch as an aid to approximate timing, indicate the opening and closing music, words of the dialogue, and sound effects on the storyboard.

Step 2 — Bar Sheet

Now do a close time analysis of all elements of your proposed sound track, including pauses between sounds. Use a stopwatch and break down the different sounds in half-second segments so that you know exactly when the music starts and stops; how long a character waits until he or she speaks; how many words and syllables are spoken, for how long; when the ceiling caves in, and so on.

This detailed "synopsis" is recorded on a *bar sheet* to guide you when recording. The bar sheet (Figure 112) has four horizontal bars on which are written:

Action — The times in the film when specific actions begin and end. The space for recording this should be larger than in the other bars, because two or more actions often take place simultaneously. You need space for notations.

Dialogue — When oral sounds begin and end. Words and syllables must be accurately timed to aid you in making later lip-sync drawings and allotting frames to them. Figure 120 in Chapter 16 shows the number of spoken words you can get into a given number of frames, and vice-versa.

Sound Effects (SFX) — When things go bump in the night, for example. Some SFX may be lengthy, like the purr of an auto engine or the wail of a fire siren. Others are instantaneous biffs, bams, and pows.

Music — Indications must be made when the background music starts and stops. Points at which the volume should logically rise or fall, or where particular musical beats occur, are indicated on the bar. Cuts, fades, and other camera effects can

be synchronized with these to improve your film's effectiveness.

Note in the sample bar sheet that the horizontal bars are intersected by vertical lines, each representing the passage of one second in time. This speeds and helps clarify interpretation of the bar sheet information, so include the vertical lines when you make your own. There are other versions of bar sheets, but all follow this general pattern. Develop a version that suits you best.

You'll need quite a number of these sheets — enough to document 360 half-seconds for every three minutes of projected film, placed end to end, would reach from here to the popcorn machine in the lobby and back. Rather than rule bars on all those sheets, turn a sheet of typing paper so its longest sides are horizontal and rule two or three segments of bar sheet on it. Then make enough photocopies to fill your needs.

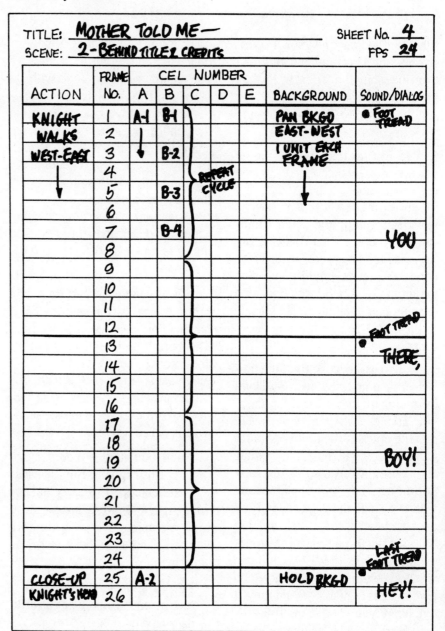

Fig. 113 *A sample dope sheet. This segment covers the same action and sound as that shown in the bar sheet (Figure 112).*

132

Fig. 114 *Examples of "instant" sounds. Because they coincide with visible actions and can be timed accordingly, these special sound effects are sometimes added after the action has been filmed.*

Step 3 — Recording

With your bar sheet as a guide, get all the sounds onto tape. You may have to be all the actors in the cast of characters, speaking the lines to get the timing right and setting the tempo for the tape. Enlist the aid of a friend to do the sound effects — like popping a cork, or slamming a door, or groaning (as when the teacher announces a test). Someone must handle the music, too.

Step 4 — Tape to Film

Next transfer the taped sound to a sound track on film. You'll have to send the tape to a processing lab for this. Send along a note that you want it on magnetic tape and remind them to provide at least 100 frames of leader at each end.

(Some animators, long in the business, prefer film with an *optical sound track* at this stage. The squiggly lines on the optical track can be "read" by an experienced film editor, recognizing voice, music, and other kinds of sound by what he or she sees. This takes a great deal of experience, however, so stick to magnetic tracks for now.)

Step 5 — The Dope Sheet

To this point in this chapter, we have been principally concerned with the *time* needed for sounds and actions on the film. Now, we turn to dealing with the *number of frames* each element requires. We are approaching the point where drawings for the film are prepared.

With the sound track back from the lab, a professional would now rely on two devices — a *sound reader* and a *synchronizer* — to obtain an accurate count of the number of frames required for each sound or voice or bit of music on the track. We're not so well equipped, so it's back to the bar sheet for us. A stopwatch and the sound track are near at hand to doublecheck the next step.

Using the bar sheet as your guide, now prepare a new information sheet that concentrates on the visual aspects of your film. It's called the dope sheet — or exposure sheet in polite circles — and will serve as your step-by-step guide for (1) the type and number of animation cels that must be drawn and (2) the sequence and frequency for photographing each cel.

The preparation of a dope sheet was explained in Chapter 11 (Figure 69 on page 93). A section of a dope sheet is shown again in Figure 113, this time with the DIALOGUE col-

133

umn filled in. The dialogue syllables on the bar sheet, now confirmed by the sound track, have been transferred to the dialogue column of the dope sheet. Use this information when you draw and number the various lip movements on animation cels. With all columns of the dope sheet filled in and checked, it's time to get to the drawing board.

Step 6 — Drawing the Animation

The hundreds of drawings needed for the animation cels and backgrounds are now prepared, following the exact instructions on the dope sheet. This is no time for flashes of creativity. The sound track is already established and timed. If you stray from the frame count on the dope sheet, your final product will be sorely out of sync.

Step 7 — Filming the Artwork

Again, it is important to follow the frame-by-frame instructions on the dope sheet when making the individual exposures that make up a complete film.

Step 8 — Married Print

The sound and visual animation finally get together on one film in this step. Send both the undeveloped animation film and the film bearing the sound track to the lab with instructions to combined them in what film-makers call the *married print*.

Optional Step 9 — Special Sounds

After the original sound track has been made and the animation has been drawn and photographed, you can still add certain sounds to your film. These usually are limited to the instantaneous ones such as the thud of a dropped book, a gunshot, exploding bubble gum, and the like. You can synchronize them with the visible action at the last, because you can see in exactly which frames they occur (Figure 114).

To do this, send off your undeveloped animation film without the film bearing the original sound track. When the developed animation is returned, arrange a special recording session for the extra sounds to be added. Assemble (1) the noise-makers, (2) a tape recorder (preferably the one used to make the original track), and (3) a projector for the animation film.

When all is set to go, start both the projector and the tape recorder. Make the appropriate special sound effects at the instances when the corresponding action appears on the screen (you may have to rehearse this several times). Your greatest problem will

be devising some method of muting the sound made by the film projector so that it won't be picked up on the tape. One suggestion is to have the projector in an adjacent room, beaming the pictures through a glass panel in the door.

When your extra recording session is completed and you are satisfied that the special sound effects are in sync with the animation and the original sound track, send all three off to the lab for processing for your long anticipated married print.

IMPORTANT: It is imperative that you let the lab know at exactly what point on the leader or at what frame on the animation film the sound should start. They will then adjust the final master sound track so that it begins 26 frames ahead of the beginning of the visual part of the film. This gives the sound track time to thread its way through the projector (Figure 115) to reach the *excitor*, which produces the sound. Thus, the sound and corresponding action are projected simultaneously.

NOW HEAR THIS

Here are some additional time- and labor-saving thoughts regarding synchronous sound.

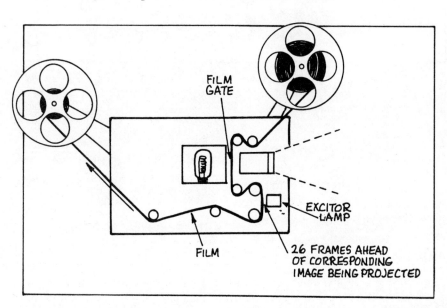

Fig. 115 This cross-section of a projector shows why a sound on the sound track must be 26 frames ahead of the corresponding action that is projected on the screen.

FILM GATE

EXCITOR LAMP

FILM

26 FRAMES AHEAD OF CORRESPONDING IMAGE BEING PROJECTED

- As a beginner, you may be excused (for a time) if you simply avoid marrying a sound track to the animation film. Try, for starters, recording the sound track on quarter-inch tape, then devise a way to time the start-up of your projector and tape player so that the video and audio portions will run in a reasonable synchronous manner.

- An even simpler, bare-bones version of this is to do animation with no sound except background music played separately. Just set your stereo or cassette player going at the appropriate time and sit back and enjoy. Even the dullest silent film can be enhanced in this fashion, as any former piano player in an old-fashioned movie house will tell you.

- Unless you're willing to take particular care in preparing your bar sheet and timing the subsequent animation, try to select background music of a general nature — a steady, repeated tempo with no particular accents or excursions into left field.

- It may not save you time, but you can avoid a lot of trouble by paying close attention to laws regarding copyrighted material. Commercial tapes and record albums and music you may have re-recorded from broadcasts cannot generally be used indiscriminately. Even recorded classical music is not copyright free, because you must first obtain the consent of the orchestra that recorded it. It is best to search out the lists of uncopyrighted material (ask your local radio station). Try being your own composer-musician or enlist the aid of talented friends.

- Stylize, even exaggerate, sound effects and voices; they will be more in harmony with your stylized animation. Don't go to the trouble of imitating the real thing when easier-to-produce sounds may work even better. Old cars are funnier if they make funny noises. Ferocious lions are fearsomely funnier when they meow like kittens.

- Use off-screen sounds for selected special effects. A waiter with a teetering armload of dishes can bring a laugh if the crash of breaking plates is heard *after* he totters out of sight. If he drops them in full view, your audience will be inclined to sympathy instead, and you'll have a lot of extra animation drawings to do.

- There are devices available that will transfer sound from quarter-inch tape to a magnetic or optical strip on either Super 8 or 16mm film. The cost of these is such that most amateur and semi-pro animators have the service done by a processing lab. If you have a super budget, however, you might look into investing in one of the new Super 8 projectors that can both record and play back sound.

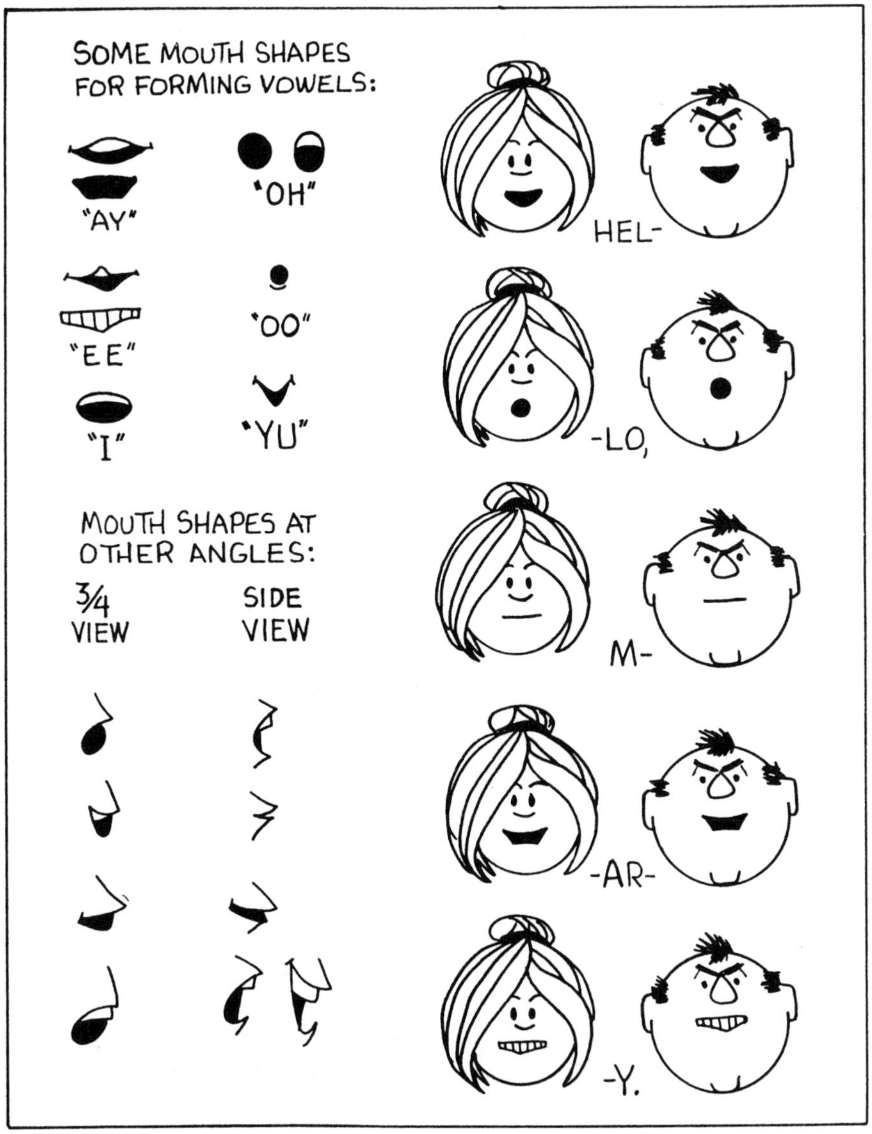

Fig. 116 Some typical mouth shapes used in animation to form speech sounds. As can be seen by the drawings of the girl and man, the same mouth shapes work for all types and ages of characters.

A thin strip of magnetic recording tape is attached to the edge of the film. You can record your sound track on this after the animation is completed and processed. Best of all, if the sync doesn't sync to your satisfaction, you can wipe the track and record again and again until it's right.

ADDING SOUND TO SCRATCH-ON FILMS

Here we go back to Chapter 6 and the experiments in scratching and drawing on film. If you've promoted yourself to a higher grade of animation, just sit this section out.

There are no hard and fast rules for creating sound for scratch-on films, just as there are none for doing the visual part. The whole process is usually a personal experience in creativity. The key word is *experiment*.

As was pointed out earlier, 16mm and 35mm films, and some of the newer Super 8 film, have narrow sound tracks along one side of the picture area (see Figure 30 on page 36). They don't give you much space to work in, but by drawing in the sound track area of clear film or scratching, scraping, or punching the track of an opaque film, you can produce a variety of weird and wonderful sounds.

Since the video part of this hands-on film process is usually a rhythmic visual pattern, the accompanying sound should have a harmonious rhythm also. The nature of the sounds in that rhythm depends on how you draw or scratch on the film.

Perhaps the best advice is to get yourself a test length of film and experiment. Draw short sections of different types of markings in the sound track area, each spanning about a second (24 frames) of projection time. Leave gaps between them so that you can tell them apart when

---

LIP SYNC

As you can imagine, putting synchronous dialogue onto a sound track and film is a laborious process. It calls for infinite care in analyzing the track and preparing corresponding animation. So, before wading into lip sync, look for alternatives. Here are some suggestions:

- Before recording, review your storyboard and/or script and see if the amount of dialogue can be reduced. Too much talk makes an animated film boring anyway, especially in a medium featuring action.

- Find spots where actions will replace spoken words. A shake of the head can often serve as well as an audible "No." A shrug says, "I couldn't care less."

- Use "off-stage" voices as they are used in regular stage plays. Voice-over lines spoken before or after a character is on the screen don't require lip-sync drawings.

You will discover other ways to reduce the amount of work involved in lip sync. But the most important one is to remember that you don't have to animate every vowel and consonant that comes down the sound track. If you try to be too realistic, you will achieve just the opposite effect. Excessively detailed lip movements result in what appears to be forced, unnatural speech, not at all like the mealy-mouthed Slurvian in which most people converse.

Create instead, a few representative mouth shapes that imitate speech sounds. Some animators prefer to stress vowels; others opt for consonants. Take your choice, but don't get bogged down trying to use both.

Stand before a mirror and study the shapes your own mouth makes when you say a variety of speech sounds. They will be similar to the standard shapes used by many animators (Figure 116). Adapt these to your own cartooning style, noting that some of the shapes serve for more than one sound. They are also repeated many times in normal speech. This means your lip-sync chores can be further simplified through heavy use of animation cycles. The viewer's eye is less concerned with the shape of the mouth than with the mouth's movement in time with the dialogue. As proof of this, the mouth movements of this century's most successful ventriloquist's dummy, Charlie McCarthy, are simply an open and shut case.

---

you run the film through a projector. Here are some of the things you'll learn:

- A series of closely-spaced horizontal marks (ladder-like lines on the sound track) will result in a vibrating sound ranging from a hum to a stutter. Closely spaced

lines produce a high-pitched hum. Thick lines produce a louder sound (Figure 117).

- You can produce steady hums from shrill to low by sticking narrow strips of patterned Zipatone or other brands of adhesive screens on the film track.

- Shapes, such as squares, circles, triangles, or just blobs, also will produce pops, bangs, and other sounds. They differ slightly according to their shapes and sizes and how you space them along the track. Working with opaque or colored film, you can punch geometric holes to make a sound track.

MUSICAL TIMING

In music, as you probably know, each musical note indicates a sound pitch as well as a space in time. Thus, you can actually devise shapes that produce variously pitched notes and, by careful spacing, create a desired rhythm. Assuming that your film is to be projected 24 frames per second, the table (Figure 118) shows how to space out the beats on the sound track.

Psst! When you draw or scratch the sound track on the film you intend to show, don't forget to start marking the sound 26 frames ahead of the start of the visual portion.

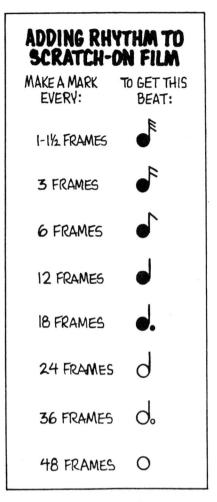

ADDING RHYTHM TO SCRATCH-ON FILM

MAKE A MARK EVERY:	TO GET THIS BEAT:
1-1½ FRAMES	♪
3 FRAMES	♪
6 FRAMES	♪
12 FRAMES	♩
18 FRAMES	♩.
24 FRAMES	♩
36 FRAMES	♩.
48 FRAMES	○

Fig. 118 You can scratch or paint on a rhythmic beat too.

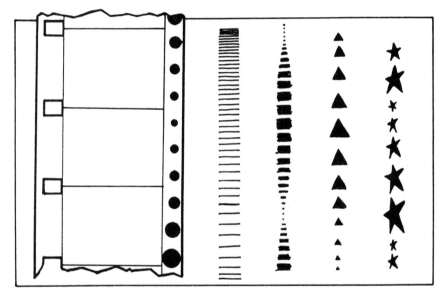

Fig. 117 These greatly enlarged scratches and doodles show some ways to add sound directly to film. For example, closely spaced thin lines at the top of the ladder-like column of scratches will produce a shrill whine; the wider spacing results in a lower hum. The heavier the line or larger the dot, the more the sound is amplified.

16

PRODUCTION NOTES

Just about everyone has a bottom desk drawer or a box in a closet for keeping odds and ends. They're the type of things that you have no use for at present, but feel they might, just might, come in handy someday. Some will.

This final chapter, then, is the bottom drawer of this book about planning and producing film animation. It's a collection of miscellany shoved aside earlier to avoid cluttering the explanation. Nevertheless, you'll find some of the information, tips, and illustrations to be of value, because they are production notes that will:

- Provide *general information* to make you a little wiser about animation.

- Help you *avoid problems*.

- Help you *save time*.

You may find the following to be a rather random arrangement. But that's how you'll be using the information, anyway.

GENERAL INFORMATION

Timing — All instructions in this book are based on a presumed projection speed of 24 fps. Some of the newer Super 8 cameras and corresponding projectors can be operated with sound at 18 fps. If you use such equipment, take the slower projection speed into account when planning animation sequences and sound. The mathematical conversion from 24 to 18 fps should not be difficult.

Also see the projection timing table (Figure 119).

Timing Objects — When manipulating the movements in three-dimensional animation, always remember that the size of an object can influence the impression of the speed at which it moves. For example, an object 2 inches (5cm) wide moved 1/4 inch (6mm) each frame will seem to move more slowly than a 1/4-inch wide object moved 1/4 inch each frame. This visual illusion occurs even though it takes the same time to get both objects from one side of the screen to the other.

Film Selection — Consult with your film supply dealer before purchasing film, explaining your animation stand setup, the lights used, and the type of artwork or objects you are shooting. Some animators recommend a slow film for completely black-and-white artwork, a medium speed stock for normal black-and-white with intermediate tones of gray, and ASA 100 or ASA 125 color film for full color work. Your personal need may be slightly different, so get expert advice.

Color or Black-and-White? — Before deciding to work with either type of film, check the prices of films and the cost of processing them. You may be surprised to find in many cases there is no cost advantage in working with black-and-white.

Shutter Speeds — Many animators working with Super 8 and 16mm film find a shutter speed of 1/30

PROJECTION TIMING		24 fps				18 fps
TYPE OF FILM	35MM	16MM	8MM	SUPER 8	SUPER 8
NO. OF FRAMES PER 1 FOOT OF FILM	16	40	80	72	72
NO. OF FRAMES PROJECTED IN 1 MINUTE	1,440	1,440	1,440	1,440	1,080
FEET OF FILM PROJECTED IN 1 MINUTE	90	36	18	20	14.72

Fig. 119 Use this table to help plan your film and estimate the amount of film you will need.

second to be satisfactory. This is not an absolute rule, however. It depends on your lighting, the film, and other factors.

Editing — One consolation in animation's single-frame shooting is that there isn't the great quantity of wasted film that generally results in live-action filming. Hence there is relatively little editing to do. Animators do edit, however, to:

• Rearrange segments of action

• Shorten a segment, often by changing a wipe to a simple cut

• Delete unwelcome things on the film (lint, out-of-focus frames, even your big fat thumb!)

• Eliminate jiggle.

If you anticipate doing much editing, borrow or purchase a *splicer*. It will cut your film smooth and square and will ensure the correct spacing of sprocket holes.

Correcting Filming Errors — If you make a mistake while shooting, close the shutter and expose about a dozen frames (they'll be solid black when the film is developed). Then reshoot the sequence, beginning at the point just before the mistake was made or at an earlier point where a cut was made from a previous scene to the present one. The black frames will give you a handle for use when at the editing bench.

Field of Vision — To help yourself along, make a *field chart* (Figure 121). The fields used in animation generally range from 1 through 12, the numbers indicating horizontal inches (2.54cm). Thus, a 3-field is 3 inches (7.62cm) wide and approximately 2 ½ inches (6.36cm) high. The field chart is fastened to or drawn directly on the baseboard. It is a handy, time-saving, and indispensable device that can be used directly on the animation stand or earlier as a reference when planning storyboards or compiling dope sheets. For example, when you write "zoom in" on a dope sheet, specifically indicate to what field (6-field, 3-field, etc.), and you'll eliminate doubts when working with the camera later on.

AVOIDING PROBLEMS

Production Estimate — Before starting your first and each subsequent film, prepare a production cost list (Figure 122). It will let you know in advance what materials and outside services you will need, what you will have to pay for, and how much they will cost. This may result in scaling down — or even adding to — a project.

Proper Exposure — When you set the stage for a new scene in three-dimensional animation, or put new artwork on the stand for cel animation, you should check to determine the proper exposure before shooting. But even if you do this frequently, you may wind up with inconsistent lighting in your total film. Too many factors are at work (Figure 123). The way to help ensure consistency of exposure throughout the film is to establish a mean or standard light reading right at the start. Write it down and refer to it as you make changes and recheck the exposure.

Dimming — Use your light meter *frequently* to maintain the proper exposure. Lamps tend to age with use, though the human eye may not detect the dimming effect.

Zoom Speed — When plotting zooms, remember that there often is a difference between the actual speed of a zoom and the impression the viewer gets. If you use 48 frames, for example, to zoom from a 12-field to a 2-field, and the same number of frames to zoom from a 12-field down to a 6, the latter will appear slower. Its ratio is 2:1 while the faster ratio is 6:1. The ratios must especially be considered when you are working with a zoom that must slow in and slow out.

Color Retention — Because of persistence of vision, the eye of the viewer will retain the color of a projected frame as well as the drawing of the action. The dominant color of each frame affects the color of succeeding frames. If you make quick cuts from bold or dark colors to light, bright ones (or vice versa), the true colors of the following frames will be momentarily obscured. Plan the colors of a film for total effect rather than frame by frame.

Reducing Shadows — When combining photos and drawings in artwork, a technique often used in titling, have your photoprints made on single-weight paper. This will reduce unwanted shadows around the edges when the photos are cut and pasted to the rest of the art.

Backgrounds — Try to keep your backgrounds reasonably simple and the colors muted to provide greater impact for the actions in front of them. Characters can get lost in overly busy backgrounds (Figure 124).

Inking and Opaquing — Problems with inking and opaquing on acetate cels (sometimes the right materials are not available) can be eliminated by introducing cutouts into cel animation. Draw the animation figures on very thin paper, cut them out with an X-acto knife, and attach them to blank cels with rubber cement. Entire animated films have been done with this method. The outlines of the figures must be fairly simple; otherwise, the cutting and pasting become a time-consuming operation.

Power Source — If you use the ad hoc method of having sound on a tape separate from the film and projector (mentioned in the previous chapter), be certain that your projector and tape player are both plugged in to the same power source. Electric power may differ slightly from one outlet to another, even in the same room. If operated from separate sources, your carefully timed picture and sound may drift out of sync. Of course, this is mentioned on the assumption that you'll use a single outlet when recording the sound to go with the projected visuals.

Extra Print — When your film is completed, processed, and deemed satisfactory, have a duplicate print made. It will be your safety net when the original print begins to scratch and tatter.

FILM CONVERSION TABLE

TIME (Seconds)	FRAMES	FEET 35mm	FEET 16mm	FEET 8mm	FEET Super 8	MAXIMUM WORDS
1	24	1.5	.6	.3	.33	2
2	48					4
3	72					7
4	96					9
5	120					11
6	144					13
7	168					15
8	192					18
9	216					20
10	240	15.0	6.0	3.0	3.3	22
11	264					24
12	288					26
13	312					28
14	336					30
15	360					33
16	384					35
17	408					37
18	432					39
19	456					41
20	480	30.0	12.0	6.0	6.6	44
21	504					46
22	528					48
23	552					50
24	576					52
25	600					55
26	624					57
27	648					59
28	672					61
29	696					63
30	720	45.0	18.0	9.0	10.0	65
31	744					67
32	768					70
33	792					72
34	816					74
35	840					76
36	864					78
37	888					80
38	912					82
39	936					85
40	960	60.0	24.0	12.0	13.2	87
41	984					89
42	1008					92
43	1032					94
44	1056					96
45	1080					98
46	1104					100
47	1128					102
48	1152					104
49	1176					106
50	1200	75.0	30.0	15.0	16.5	108
51	1224					110
52	1248					112
53	1272					115
54	1296					117
55	1320					119
56	1344					122
57	1368					124
58	1392					126
59	1426					128
60	1440	90.0	36.0	18.0	20.0	130
2 min.	2880	180.0	72.0	36.0	39.6	260
3 min.	4320	270.0	108.0	54.0	59.4	390
4 min.	5760	360.0	144.0	72.0	79.2	520
5 min.	7200	450.0	180.0	90.0	99.0	650
10 min.	14400	900.0	360.0	180.0	198.0	1300
20 min.	28800	1800.0	720.0	360.0	396.0	2600
30 min.	43200	2700.0	1080.0	540.0	594.0	3900
60 min.	86400	5400.0	2160.0	1080.0	1188.0	7800

Fig. 120 This table will help you plan animation to fit a given number of words ... or to write dialogue limited to a given number of frames.

SAVING TIME

Almost every chapter in this book has dwelt at length on shortcuts for the animator. Some examples: double and triple framing, skipping frames entirely, limited animation, cel cycles, panning cels, panning backgrounds, the buddy system, and more. Even time-consuming chores like making test exposures and preparing storyboards, field charts, bar sheets, dope sheets, pan charts, and templates can save you many hours in the long run.

Here are two more time-savers that may be useful to you:

Film Loops — After making and processing a short length of test footage to check certain aspects of your work, it is annoying to have to repeatedly re-thread the film in the projector for thorough study. You can avoid this simply by splicing the ends of the film together after it is threaded in the projector. The loop you make will run without interruption, letting you view the test frames again and again.

Drawing to Scale — A problem in animating a figure that moves directly toward you or recedes into the distance is calculating the amount of increase or reduction in the size of each drawing in the cycle. Even more difficult is making the figure retain an identical appearance as it expands or shrinks. A time-saving and accurate way of doing this is to make the drawings on graph paper, using successively larger or smaller square as guides (Figure 125), then transferring the drawings to cels.

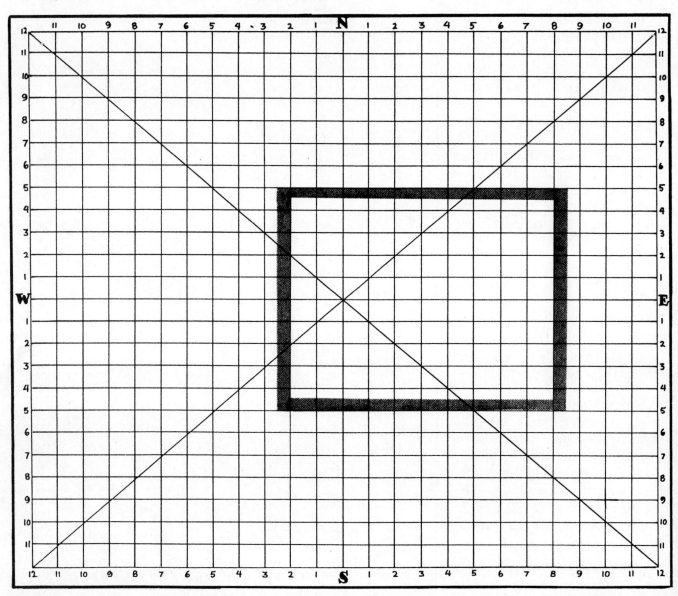

Fig. 121 A hand-drawn field chart (not actual size). This one is drawn for a field of vision 12 inches wide. The shaded rectangle indicates the area that would be filmed if the camera were focused for a 5 field and were panned slightly to the right.

TEAMWORK IS FAST AND FUN

In many schools where art students are experimenting with film animation, the usual procedure is to form "production teams" to write, plan, record, illustrate, and photograph individual films.

A team may consist of two, three, or as many as six students. Everybody gets into the act when the script is conceived and written. Then individual tasks are assigned for storyboarding, charting, creating characters, in-betweening, and so on. The same procedure is followed in the recording phase.

During the actual shooting, one person handles the camera, a second makes cel or artwork changes (or moves the objects in three-dimensional shooting), another, guided by the dope sheet, directs the activity. The assignments are rotated periodically, or with each succeeding film, to give everyone experience in doing all the things necessary to create animation.

Students also enjoy the freewheeling creativity of drawing or scratching directly on film. This can be done by teams also. Seated at long or circular tables, each artist is assigned a measured number of frames on a continuous length of film.

Team members work independently, none knowing what his or her neighbors are doing. Or they may all be given copies of a simple figure, the "star" of the film, and be left to animate the figure according to individual inventiveness.

Working in this manner, an entire reel of film can be covered with animation and the results shown on a screen in much less time than if one person took on the job. The teamwork films are great learning experiences, often with surprising results, and always fun!

PLANNING AND BUDGETING CHECKLIST

	ESTIMATED COST
EQUIPMENT	
Animation Stand	_____
Camera	_____
Tripod	_____
Cable Release	_____
Lights	_____
Light Box	_____
Tape Recorder (¼")	_____
Projector	_____
Screen	_____
Film Splicer	_____
SUPPLIES	
Film Stock, Leader	_____
Animation Paper	_____
Cels	_____
Inks, Paints	_____
Brushes, Pens, Misc.	_____
Register Pegs	_____
Field Guide	_____
Extra Light Bulbs	_____
Props	_____
¼" Recording Tape	_____
Magnetic Recording Stock	_____
Cotton Gloves	_____
Felt Marker	_____
Splicing Tape	_____
Extra Reels, Cans	_____
OUTSIDE SERVICES	
Film Processing	_____
Sound Track on Film	_____
Married Print	_____
Optical Effects	_____

Fig. 122 *Even "amateur" filming costs money. This list will help you gauge your costs. It does not contain many items and services that professional animators use.*

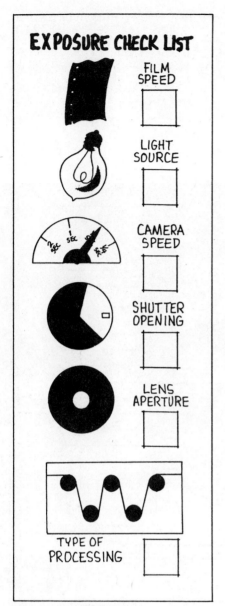

EXPOSURE CHECK LIST

FILM SPEED ☐

LIGHT SOURCE ☐

CAMERA SPEED ☐

SHUTTER OPENING ☐

LENS APERTURE ☐

TYPE OF PROCESSING ☐

Fig. 123 Better safe than sorry. Run down this checklist every time you resume or make changes in your filming.

Fig. 124 Keep it simple. An overly-busy background obscures your characters and the action you want to show.

FADE OUT

Alan Cleave, a British animator, once likened the making of an animation film to a walk through a long, straight tunnel. There are times it seems you'll never reach that wee light at the end of the tunnel. But if you keep plugging, it does seem to grow larger until, at last, you emerge in the full light with a completed film in your projector. It's worth working and waiting for. Perhaps this book will help you through this most interesting tunnel. As was pointed out at the beginning, it is intended to make you knowledgeable in the fundamental and inexpensive techniques of animation. There is still much more to be learned, and it is hoped you have acquired an enthusiasm to go on. As Rembrandt said when he put down his paint brushes and took up etching: "I have just scratched the surface."

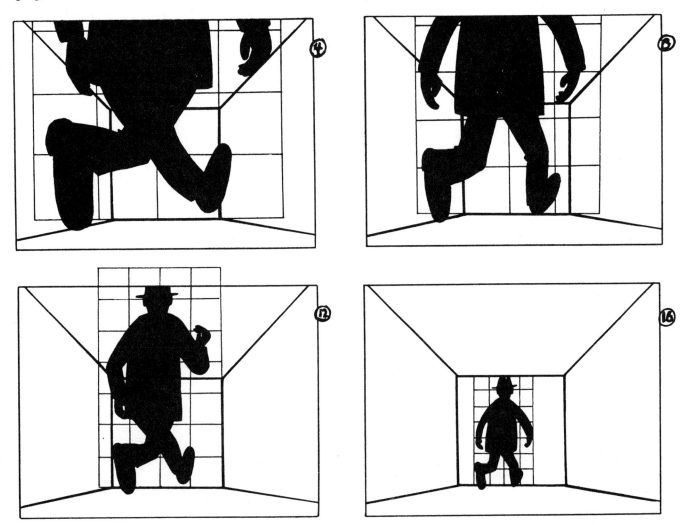

Fig. 125 Use graph paper or a hand-drawn grid of squares to keep the proportions of a figure in scale as it advances toward or recedes from the camera. In the frames above, the animator drew a basic walking figure in a grid four squares wide and seven squares high. The size of the squares was successively reduced to keep the walking man always in the correct proportion. The grids, of course, were not included in the final tracings on cels.

BIBLIOGRAPHY

Basic Titling and Animation for Motion Pictures. Rochester, NY: Eastman Kodak Co., 1972.

Bourgeois, Jacques, Andrea Hobson, and Mark Hobson. *Simple Film Animation With and Without a Camera.* New York: Sterling Publishing Co., 1979. (Also published as two separate books. The Bourgeois portion features hand-drawn and scratch-off films. The other, describing the work of the teenage Hobson brothers, concentrates on animation with cutouts.)

Cleave, Alan. *Cartoon Animation for Everyone.* Watford, England: Argus Books Ltd., 1977. (Good basic information on cel and cutout animation.)

Doing the Media: A Portfolio of Activities and Resources. New York: The Center for Understanding the Media, 1972. (Briefly describes classroom projects for teaching students how to produce animation and live-action films. Mainly for elementary grades.)

Hurrell, Ron. *Manual of Television Graphics.* New York: Van Nostrand Reinhold Co., 1973.

Kinsey, Anthony. *How to Make Animated Movies.* New York: Viking Press, 1970.

Laybourne, Kit. *The Animation Book.* New York: Crown Publishers, Inc. (By a teacher/animator. The most comprehensive book for beginners in this listing.)

Levitan, Eli L. *An Alphabetical Guide to Motion Pictures, Television, and Video Production.* New York: McGraw-Hill Book Co., 1970. (Encyclopedia format. Good for quick reference on details.)

Levitan, Eli L. *Handbook of Animation Techniques.* New York: Van Nostrand Reinhold Co., 1979. (Features professional animation techniques for television commercials.)

Perisic, Zoran. *The Focalguide to Shooting Animation.* London: Focal Press, 1978.

Roberts, Kenneth R., and Win Sharples, Jr. *A Primer of Film-Making.* New York: Pegasus, Division of Bobbs-Merrill, 1971.

da Silva, Raul. *The World of Animation.* Rochester, NY: Eastman Kodak Co., 1979.

Trojanski, John, and Louis Rockwood. *Making it Move.* Dayton, OH: Pflaum/Standard, 1973.

GLOSSARY

ACETATE — Cellulose triacetate, a clear plastic material available in sheet form for artwork and overlays. Also available frosted on one side of the sheet.

ACTION — The events and, more specifically, the actual movements in an animated film.

ADD-ONS — Portions of the line and/or color added to a drawing or a title word under the camera to complete the drawing or word.

ANIMATED ZOOM — A movement toward or away from the viewer by the use of artwork rather than the camera. Several drawings of an object are made in different sizes and are photographed in series to give the illusion that the object is coming nearer or receding.

ANIMATION — Collectively, the entire process of creating apparent movement of inanimate objects and drawings by making progressive changes in their positions and photographing each change. The term also refers to the end result projected on a screen.

ANIMATION DISC — A circular disc with attached register pegs, which is inserted in the drawing board or baseboard and can be rotated to any angle. Its principal use is in the drawing and photographing of diagonal movements.

ANIMATION STAND — A unit designed especially to hold and photograph animation artwork. The stand includes a baseboard, registration devices, platen, lighting equipment, and camera.

ANIMATOSCOPE, FANATO-SCOPE, FILOSCOPE, PHENA-KISTOSCOPE, PRAXINOSCOPE, STROBOSCOPE, THAUMA-TROPE, ZOETROPE — Some of the hundreds of mechanical and optical devices preceding the development of modern motion picture projectors.

ARMATURE — A skeletal form, usually of wire, on which clay figures are sculpted for use in three-dimensional animation.

ARTWORK—Drawings, paintings, cutouts, photographs, and other graphic materials prepared for animation.

ASA NUMBER — Also called the *emulsion speed number*, this is a measure of a film's sensitivity to light. The higher the number, the more sensitive the film. The measurement is against a scale devised by the American Standards Association (ASA).

AUDIO — The sound portion of a film presentation.

BACKGROUND — Any plain, textured, or colored material, which may also have a scene painted on it, over which artwork is laid for photographing. In three-dimensional animation, the background is any illustrated, textured, or plain backdrop in front of which the animated objects are manipulated.

BACKLIGHTED JIG — A device for holding opaque film while drawing scratch-off animation. A rectangle the size of one frame is cut in the jig and a light is placed beneath the hole.

BAR SHEET — A chart, usually in four horizontal bars, prepared for analyzing the recorded sound track. The numbers of frames allotted to visual images, dialogue, music, and special effects are marked on the bars to synchronize with the sound track.

BASEBOARD — The flat surface normally at the bottom of an animation stand on which artwork is positioned for photographing. Also called a *compound*.

BLANK — A frame or series of frames on the film, which has been exposed with nothing in it.

CABLE RELEASE — A covered spring attached to the camera. It has a push button at its outer end and a central wire, which activates the camera shutter to expose one frame at a time.

CAMCORDER — A hand-held video camera. Some models have a single-frame feature that can be used for taping animation.

CEL — A rectangular sheet of transparent acetate on which animation drawings are inked and painted. Cels are usually pre-punched with holes that fit over register pegs to hold the cels in position during art preparation and photographing.

CEL LEVEL — The position of a cel in relation to the background when a group of cels is placed on the register pegs. Cel levels usually are designated by letters (A through E), A being the bottom level next to the background.

CLOSE-UP — A figure photographed from a short distance so that only a portion of it fills the frame; for example, a girl shown only from the waist up. A picture in which her head almost filled the frame would be called an *extreme close-up*. In camera directions these terms are abbreviated as CU and ECU.

COMPOSITE PRINT — A processed film containing both pictures and sound track.

COMPOUND — See BASEBOARD.

CONTINUITY — The continuing flow of action, dialogue, sound, and art style in a filmed story. A movie scriptwriter is sometimes referred to as a continuity writer.

CREDITS — Acknowledgments at the beginning or end of a film for those persons who contributed to its production.

CUT — An instantaneous change from one scene to another or from one position to another within a scene (as from a long shot to a close-up).

CUT-AWAY WIPE — The transition of scenes in which one picture is placed on top of another and thin strips of the top picture are cut away between exposures.

CUTOUT — A drawing or other type of illustration and its parts, put onto thin cardboard and cut out to be used in animation.

CYCLE — A series of animation drawings on cels, which can be repeated again and again to create a continuing action of any desired duration.

DEFINITION — The degree of clarity with which the details of a filmed image can be seen.

DEPTH OF FIELD — The distance between the nearest and farthest objects in the camera's view that remain in focus. The wider the lens is opened, the shallower will be the depth of field.

DIALOGUE — Speech, conversation, and off-screen voices recorded on the sound track or shown visually on the screen.

DISSOLVE — An optical effect in which one scene gradually fades out as a second scene simultaneously appears (fades in). A double exposure exists where the two scenes overlap.

DOCUMENTARY — An animated film or a live-action film depicting in a factual manner historical and other events or conditions. Films produced for training purposes are also called documentaries.

DOLLY — To move the camera closer to or away from the subject being photographed. The effect is the same as a zoom. In animation, dollying is done by moving the camera down and up in the animation stand. The term *dolly* comes from the wheeled dolly bearing the camera on a full-scale motion picture stage.

DOPE SHEET — A detailed chart used at the animation stand to direct shooting. It lists every frame in sequence, giving camera directions and the number and position of cels and other artwork, on the baseboard. Also called an exposure sheet.

DOUBLE FRAMING — Shooting an object, drawing, or cutout twice before changing its position.

DOUBLE PROJECTION — An early technique in magic lantern shows in which one image was projected on top of the other. This was usually done to show an image against a scenic background.

DRAG — The elongated distortion of a moving object to give the illusion of the backward pull of inertia and friction.

DROPPED SHADOW — A shadow behind or below lettering in titles to make them more legible and improve their appearance.

DRY TRANSFER LETTERING — Commercially produced alphabets that can be rubbed onto artwork. Often used in titles.

EAST, WEST, NORTH, SOUTH — Terms indicating the directions of lateral and vertical moves of artwork on the baseboard. For example, east-west is right to left.

EDITING — The assembly, arrangement, and splicing of visual frames and sound track to form a complete film.

EMULSION — The thin photosensitive coating on one side of film.

EXCITOR — Apparatus in projector that interprets messages from the sound track into sound.

EXPOSURE METER — A photo-electric device for measuring the intensity of light falling on and/or reflected from an object. It is used as an aid to determining correct lens setting. Also called a *light meter*.

EXPOSURE SHEET — See DOPE SHEET.

EXTREME CLOSE-UP — See CLOSE-UP.

EXTREMES — Drawings of an animated figure showing the positions at the start and finish of an action. Also called *key drawings*. In animation, extremes are drawn first, and the intermediate positions (in-betweens) are then added.

FADE — An optical effect achieved in the camera or in the laboratory resulting in (a) a blank film on which an image gradually appears and strengthens (fade in) or (b) a picture that gradually fades out to a blank or totally dark film.

FANATOSCOPE — See ANIMA-TOSCOPE.

FIELD — The area "seen" by the camera lens and, therefore, the area that will appear in an exposed frame. In animation, this field of vision is measured in horizontal inches. A 6-field is 6 inches (15.24cm) wide.

FIELD CHART — A graph-like sheet of numbered rectangles used to indicate the area on the baseboard within the camera's view. The chart is used in planning animation, in positioning artwork, and for plotting zooms and panning movements.

FIELD GUIDE — See FIELD CHART.

FILM SPEED — The measurement of a film's sensitivity to light as expressed by an ASA number.

FILMGATE — A device in a movie projector that opens and closes to permit projection of light through only one frame of film at a time.

FILM-HOLDING JIG — A hand-made device for holding a strip of film when making hand-drawn or scratch-off films.

FILOSCOPE — See ANIMA-TOSCOPE.

FLASH PAN — A very rapid pan away from a figure or an object. The blurred effect is often used to imply a change of time or location.

FLIP BOOK — A series of animation drawings assembled and fastened together to form a pad of paper. When they are held in the hands and riffled, an illusion of motion is achieved.

FLIPPING — A method for rapidly viewing preliminary sketches of an action to evaluate its movements. The sketches are held and released in a way similar to the manipulation of a flip book. This is not to be confused with the term *flip* used by professional animators to indicate the turning of a scene on a central axis to make a transition to another scene.

FOCUS PULL — A technique in which a title or scene is filmed in a blurred, out-of-focus manner, then gradually brought into sharp definition by adjusting the camera's focus ring. The process can be reversed, from sharp to blurred focus.

FOOTAGE — A term used in referring to the length of a segment of film.

FOREGROUND — Artwork, usually the top cel or overlay on the baseboard, which has the appearance of being in front of the principal action. In three-dimensional animation, the foreground is that area closest to the camera.

FPS — An abbreviation of frames per second.

FRAME — One picture space in the series that makes up a strip or reel of film.

FRAME COUNTER — A device on a movie camera showing the number of frames that have been exposed on a reel or cartridge of film.

FRAME-COUNTING JIG — A device for holding opaque film while scratch-off drawings are made. Regularly spaced and numbered lines along each side of the film help keep track of the position and number of frames being scratched.

F STOP — A lens setting, usually ranging from f/1.4 to f/32, signifying the relationship between the lens focal length and the diameter of the lens aperture. The larger the f stop number, the smaller the aperture.

GATE — See FILMGATE.

HELD CEL — A cel in limited animation held for several frames while the movement cels are exposed.

HOLD — The act of stopping the changes in cels and cutouts or the movement of objects in order to expose several identical frames.

IMAGE — Any single photographically obtained likeness on film.

IN-BETWEENS — The intermediate drawings made to create a smooth flow of movement between key drawings (extremes).

INKING — Tracing the lines of an animation drawing on transparent cels.

JUMPING THE PEGS — Repeating the pan to extend the duration of an action.

KEY DRAWINGS — See EXTREMES.

KINESTASIS — A quasi-animated technique in which stop-motion is used to show a rapid series of photographs, cutouts, slides, or other materials. Also see STOP-MOTION.

LAYOUT — The overall design of a scene drawn on paper, or the plan for arrangement of objects in three-dimensional animation.

LEADER — Clear or opaque film at the start and end of a reel. The leader facilitates threading film into the projector and protects the printed film in storage and handling.

LEGIBILITY — Color combinations used in titles that make it easy to discern words and pictures.

LENS APERTURE — Opening in the camera allowing light in to expose the film.

LIGHT METER — See EXPOSURE METER.

LIMITED ANIMATION — A shortcut technique used in cel animation. Only the portions of a figure that move are redrawn and used as overlays on the basic stationary cel or cels.

LIP SYNCHRONIZATION — The relationship between visual movements of the mouth to speech sounds. If they do not coincide, the film is said to be out of sync. Also called *lip sync*, for short.

LIVE-ACTION — Film sequences in which actors, scenes, and objects are filmed with a continuously running motion picture camera.

LONG SHOT — Abbreviated LS. A view from a distance in which figures and objects appear small, as opposed to a close-up in which they fill the screen.

MAGNETIC TRACK — A narrow strip on a film coated with a magnetic medium on which sound is recorded.

MARRIED PRINT — See COMPOSITE PRINT.

MEDIUM SHOT — Abbreviated MS. A figure or an object photographed at a position in between a long shot and a close-up; for example, a person whose full figure goes from the top to bottom of the screen.

METAMORPHOSIS — A technique in which an animated object gradually takes the form of another object; for example, a coil of rope that unwinds itself and forms a word or a Dr. Jekyll transformed into a Mr. Hyde.

MICKEY MOUSING — The process of matching movements precisely with the beat of music, first introduced in animation by Walt Disney.

MOVEMENT CEL — One of a series of cels used in conjunction with a held cel in limited animation.

MOVEMENT DRAWING — See MOVEMENT CEL. These are usually the in-betweens drawn to show the successive positions of a moving object or part of an object (as in leg movements).

MULTIPLE PAN — Panning movements of artwork and/or backgrounds in which two or more cels are moved in different directions or in the same direction at different speeds.

NARRATION — A speech monologue most often recorded as a voiceover by an off-screen commentator or storyteller.

OBJECT ANIMATION — Another term for three-dimensional animation in which objects, dolls, and puppets are manipulated before the camera during single-frame exposures.

ONES, TWOS, THREES — The number of frames a cel, a cutout, or an object is held without change during shooting. A cel exposed three times before substituting another cel is said to be shot "on threes." See DOUBLE FRAMING.

OPAQUING — Filling in opaque color between the inked outlines of a drawing on a cel. Opaquing is usually done on the reverse side of the cel. Also called *whiting in*.

OPTICAL SOUND TRACK — A sound track on film in which the sounds are recorded as visual patterns. In the projector, light impulses from the pattern are converted to audible sounds.

OVERLAY — A cel or piece of artwork placed over the background or other cels on the animation stand.

OVER-THE-CAMERA — A technique in which a person or object seems to enter the frame from behind and over the top of the camera.

PAN — To move the camera's field of vision horizontally or vertically. In animation, this is done by (a) moving the baseboard to which the artwork is attached or (b) moving the artwork, which has been drawn on extra lengths of paper or cels.

PAN CHART — A diagram attached to the baseboard to guide the distance and frequency of panning movements.

PANNING BACKGROUNDS — A background that is moved east-west or north-south as animation cels and cutouts are exposed in front of it. The illusion is that the animated figure is progressing in one direction or another.

PANNING CYCLES — Repeated use of a panning sequence, thus stretching out the lateral or up-and-down movement to any desired length.

PANORAMA — An extended horizontal scene drawn or painted on the background and used in panning.

PARALLAX — The apparent repositioning of an object in the field of vision caused by a viewfinder with an optical axis that is not the same as the optical axis of the camera lens. Through-the-lens viewfinders eliminate parallax.

PEG BAR — A flat strip of metal or plastic to which register pegs are attached. The peg bar is attached to a drawing board or baseboard with tape; or it is fitted into grooves cut in the boards to permit it to be moved from side to side.

PERSISTENCE OF VISION — The retention by the eye of an image for a split second after the image is removed from sight.

PHENAKISTOSCOPE — See ANIMATOSCOPE.

PIXILATION — The use of people as animated figures in single-frame photography. This technique can show humans in actions that are impossible to achieve in live-action shooting.

PLATEN — A rectangle of clear glass or plastic used to hold artwork flat on the baseboard.

POP-ONS — Words, speech balloons, and other devices that appear suddenly on the screen.

PRAXINOSCOPE — See ANIMATOSCOPE.

PRINT — A developed reel of film. Also, in still photography, a positive picture developed from a negative.

PROCESSING — The developing and printing of film, including sound tracks. This is usually done in a special photo processing lab.

PRODUCTION — Generally referring to all phases of the creation and processing of a film, or to the completed film itself.

PROJECTION — The act of transmitting a visual image on film to become a larger picture viewed on a screen or other surface.

PUSH-OFF WIPE — The transition of one picture to another. The top picture is cut into two or more segments and the pieces are moved out of the frame in opposite directions.

RAW STOCK — Unexposed film.

REGISTER — The precise positioning of successive drawings and/or cels to ensure that all are aligned when photographed. Proper registration eliminates fuzziness and jerkiness in filmed movements.

REGISTER PEGS — Small pegs of metal, plastic, or wood protruding from the surface of an animator's drawing board. Sheets of drawing paper or cels with corresponding holes are placed over the pegs to hold each sheet in register; that is, in exactly identical positions. Similar pegs are attached to the baseboard of the animation stand to hold artwork and cels in position while being photographed.

ROSTRUM — See ANIMATION STAND. (Rostrum is the term used by British animators.)

ROTOSCOPING — A recent, sophisticated technique of first filming in live-action, then tracing and coloring each frame to create an animated sequence with lifelike characteristics.

SANDWICH — Two or more cels placed one over the other on the baseboard and photographed as a single frame.

SCRATCH-OFF ANIMATION —

The technique of creating animated patterns and simple images by scratching the emulsion from opaque film. No camera is needed. Though often an elementary exercise, scratch-off has been used in making sophisticated professional animated films. The technique is also sometimes used in cel animation to eliminate portions of drawings a bit at a time for special effects. The erasures are done under the camera (also see ADD-ONS).

SCRIPT — The written version of a film, including directions for the action, dialogue, music, and sound effects.

SEQUENCE — A series of frames comprising one particular action.

SETTING — The scene is which action takes place. It may be a miniature "stage" setup in three-dimensional animation. In cel and cutout animation, the background art serves as the setting. It can be absolutely blank.

SHADOW FILM — An early form of animation. Cardboard cutouts were held in front of backlighting to cast shadows on a screen. The moving images were then photographed. (See SILHOUETTE FILM.)

SHOT — The exposure of a single frame of film.

SHUTTER — A mechanical device in cameras, which opens and shuts to expose film. Also a device in projectors that cuts off the beam of light during the instant the film is moved forward the space of one frame.

SHUTTER SPEED — The rate at which a camera lens aperture opens and closes.

SILHOUETTE FILM — A type of animated film in which cutout figures are used. The silhouetted figures appear as solid shapes on a lighter background, which may have a scene drawn on it.

SINGLE-FRAME ACTION — The ability of a motion picture camera to be stopped after exposing one frame.

SINGLE-FRAMING — Moving artwork or objects each time a frame is exposed. Also called *shooting on ones*.

SLIDE — A single sheet of glass or transparent film bearing an image for projection.

SLIDING CEL — A cel two or more times as wide as the total field under the camera. It is used to pan an image left or right across the background. Also called *panning cel*.

SLOW-IN, SLOW-OUT — The technique of obtaining lifelike movements of objects or animated drawings by starting them off slowly and gradually slowing to a stop.

SOUND EFFECTS — Sounds on the sound track from any source other than dialogue, voice-over, and background music.

SOUND READER — A device used when preparing bar sheets and in editing. The reader permits analysis and timing of dialogue and other sounds for the purpose of establishing frame counts for the visual animation.

SOUND TRACK — See MAGNETIC TRACK and OPTICAL SOUND TRACK.

SPECIAL EFFECTS — Visual gimmicks such as wipes, fades, dissolves, focus pulls, etc., obtained by manipulating the camera and/or artwork.

SPLICER — A device used to cut and join film. Its greatest advantage is that it maintains the correct spacing of sprocket holes in the film.

SPROCKETS — Projecting pins on the drive wheels in projectors and cameras. They fit into sprocket holes in film to move it forward or backward.

SQUASH — The exaggerated compression or flattening of an object, usually shown when the animated object strikes a solid surface. In some comic effects, the solid surface squashes in and not the object that strikes it.

STOP-DOWN — To reduce the opening in a camera lens aperture, thus reducing the exposure.

STOP-MOTION (KINESTASIS) — A technique using still photographs and drawings to achieve the illusion of motion, change, and/or passage of time by quick changes from one image to another. The method is also known as *filmograph* and *ikonograph*.

STORYBOARD — An abbreviated pictorial outline of a film's characters and actions prepared in the planning stage as an aid to visualizing the written script.

STRETCH — The elongation of a moving object to give the illusion of momentum or the pull of inertia. (See DRAG.)

STROBE — An unwelcome jitter or staccato movement of the projected image. It is most often caused by a faulty projector or the way the film is threaded in it. Faulty register or jiggling the camera on the animation stand may also cause strobing.

STROBOSCOPE — See ANIMATOSCOPE.

STROBOSCOPIC PHOTO — A multi-imaged picture obtained by photographing the movement of a person or an object as a precisely timed light flashes on and off.

SUBTRACTS — Portions of a drawing removed from a drawing while under the camera.

SWISH — The rapid movement of an object, usually accompanied by parallel "swish lines," to give the illusion of speed.

SYNCHRONIZATION — The precise positioning of a sound track so that it corresponds with the visual portions of the film, or vice versa.

SYNCHRONIZER — A device used by professional filmmakers to synchronize sound and visuals.

TAIL END — The final frames on a reel of film.

TEMPLATE — A thin plastic or cardboard device hinged to the baseboard to guide the positioning of an animated cutout.

THAUMATROPE — See ANIMATOSCOPE.

TITLE — Verbal information at the beginning and end of a film to give the film's name, credits, and other information. Titles can be used throughout a film, especially in documentaries and training films, to provide subheadings.

TRACING — The act of precisely transferring animation drawings to cels by inking.

TRANSITION EFFECT — Any special visual effect that accomplishes a smooth transition from one scene to another without loss of mood and continuity.

TRAVELING PEG BAR — A peg bar set into a groove in the baseboard; the bar can be moved left and right for the purpose of panning.

VIDEO — The visual portion of a film presentation, a term most often applied in television.

VIDEO CAMERA — See CAMCORDER.

VIEWFINDER — A camera component for determining the camera's field of vision. A reflex viewfinder views directly through the lens; a non-reflex viewfinder is separate from the lens and has a different optical axis. (See PARALLAX.)

VOICE-OVER — The speech of an off-screen narrator on a sound track accompanying the visual images.

WHITING IN — See OPAQUING.

WINDBACK — A facility for winding back exposed film in the camera in order to reshoot frames for dissolves, fades, and other special effects involving double exposure.

WIPE — A visual technique used to bring a scene onto the screen (wipe on) or to remove it (wipe off) over the span of several frames. Wipes are used most often to accomplish a transition from one scene to another. Wiping can be done in an extremely wide variety of shapes and movements.

ZOETROPE — See ANIMATOSCOPE.

ZOOM — Moving in or away from an object to provide a smooth enlargement or reduction in the size of the object on the screen. Zooming in brings an object closer to the viewer; zooming out moves it away. Zooms can be accomplished on the animation stand by moving the camera up or down, or by adjusting the zoom lens on a stationary camera.

Index